A DELICIOUS TREASURY OF AMERICAN TASTE

GWENDOLYN MICHEL

REFLECTIVE INK PRESS

A DELICIOUS TREASURY
OF AMERICAN TASTE

Published by
Reflective Ink Press
P.O. Box 178, Moss Landing, Ca 95039
www.reflectiveinkpress.com

ISBN 978-0-9991222-9-7
Printed in the United States of America

A DELICIOUS TREASURY OF AMERICAN TASTE

GWENDOLYN MICHEL

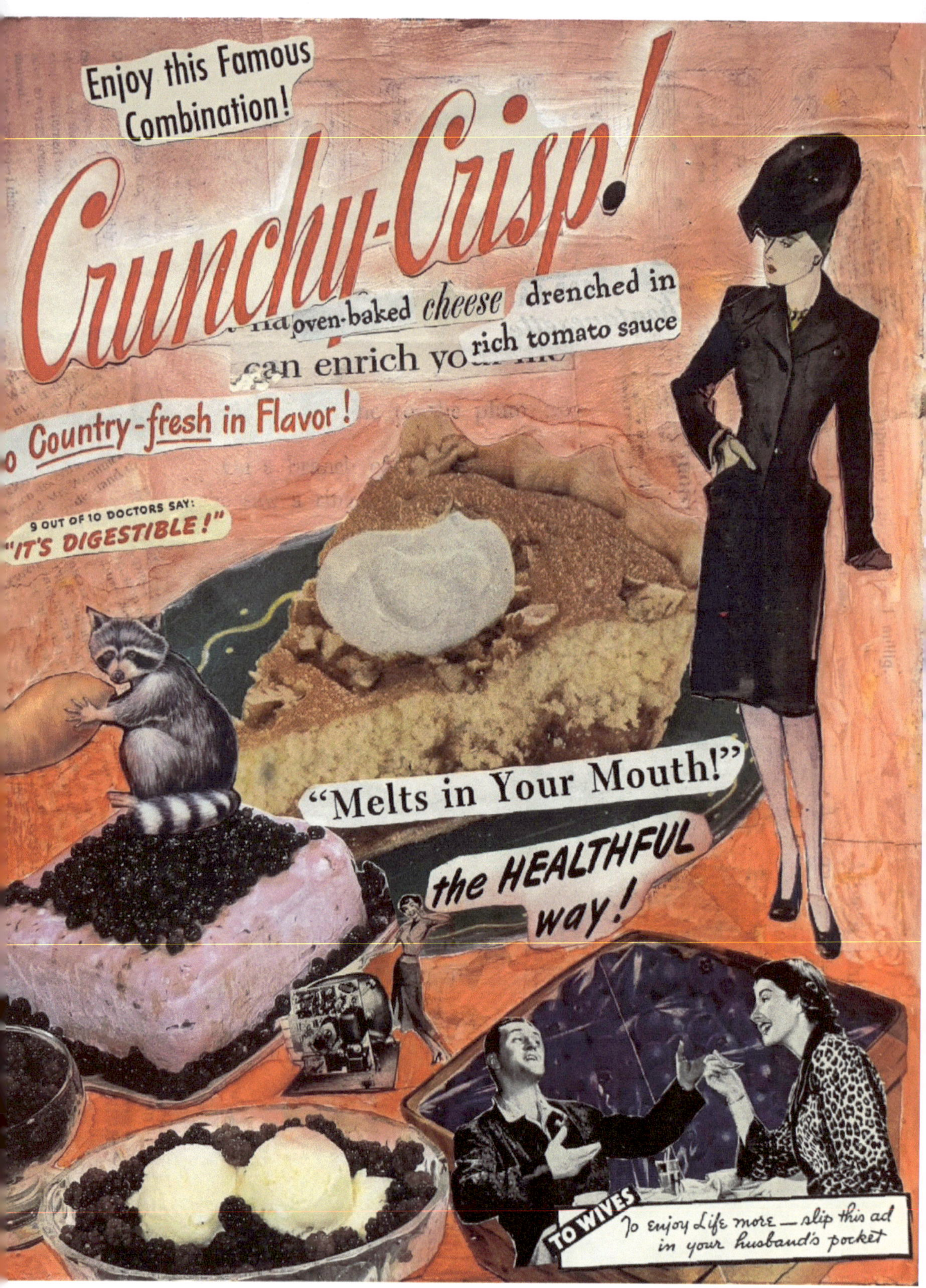

Enjoy this Famous Combination!
Crunchy-Crisp!
oven-baked cheese
drenched in
rich tomato sauce
can enrich yo
o Country-fresh in Flavor!
9 OUT OF 10 DOCTORS SAY:
"IT'S DIGESTIBLE!"
"Melts in Your Mouth!"
the HEALTHFUL way!
TO WIVES
To enjoy Life more — slip this ad in your husband's pocket

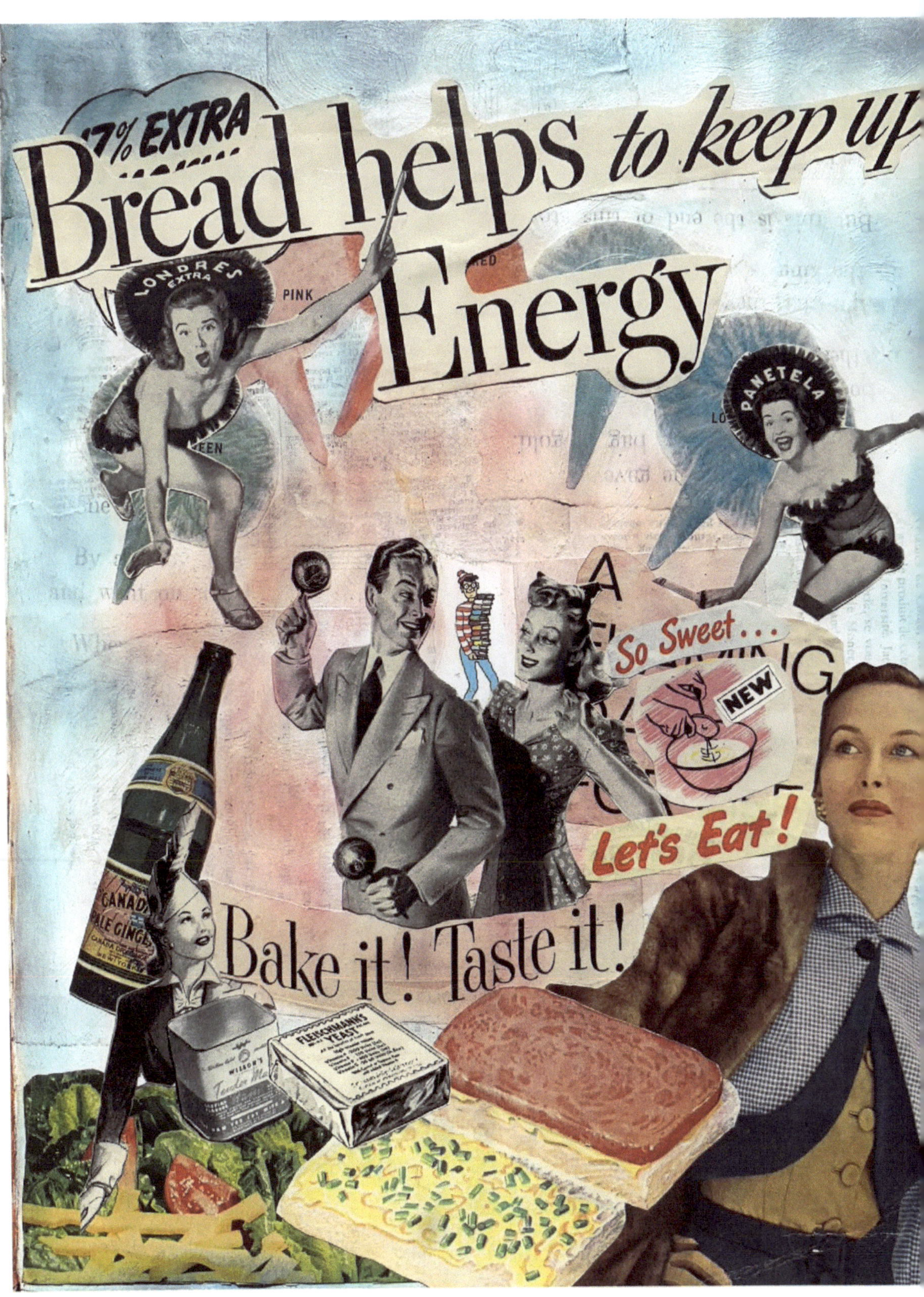
7% EXTRA
Bread helps to keep
Energy
LONDRES EXTRA
PINK
PANETELA
So Sweet...
NEW
Let's Eat!
Bake it! Taste it!
FLEISCHMANN'S YEAST

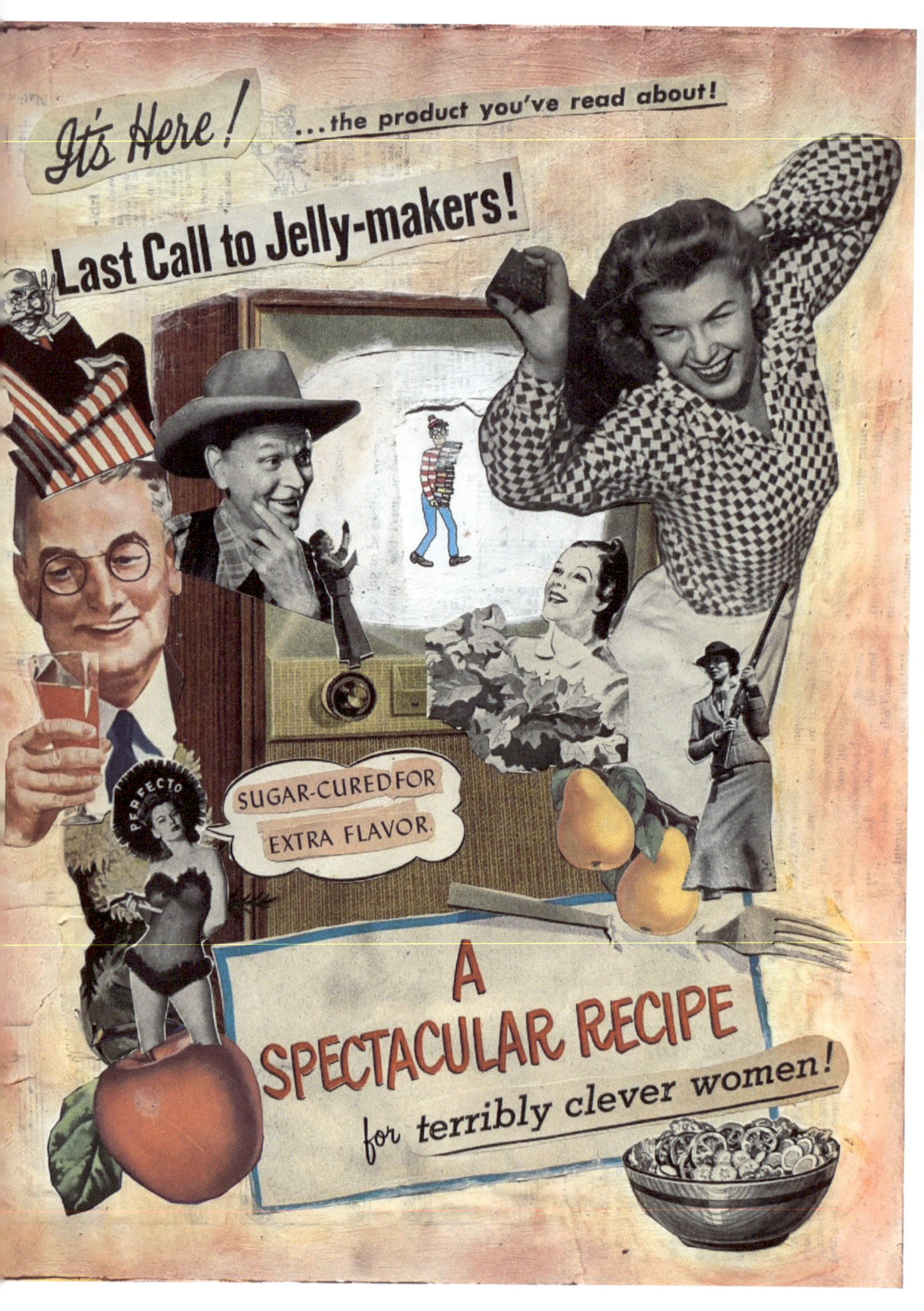
It's Here!
...the product you've read about!
Last Call to Jelly-makers!
PERFECTO
SUGAR-CURED FOR
EXTRA FLAVOR.
A
SPECTACULAR RECIPE
for terribly clever women!

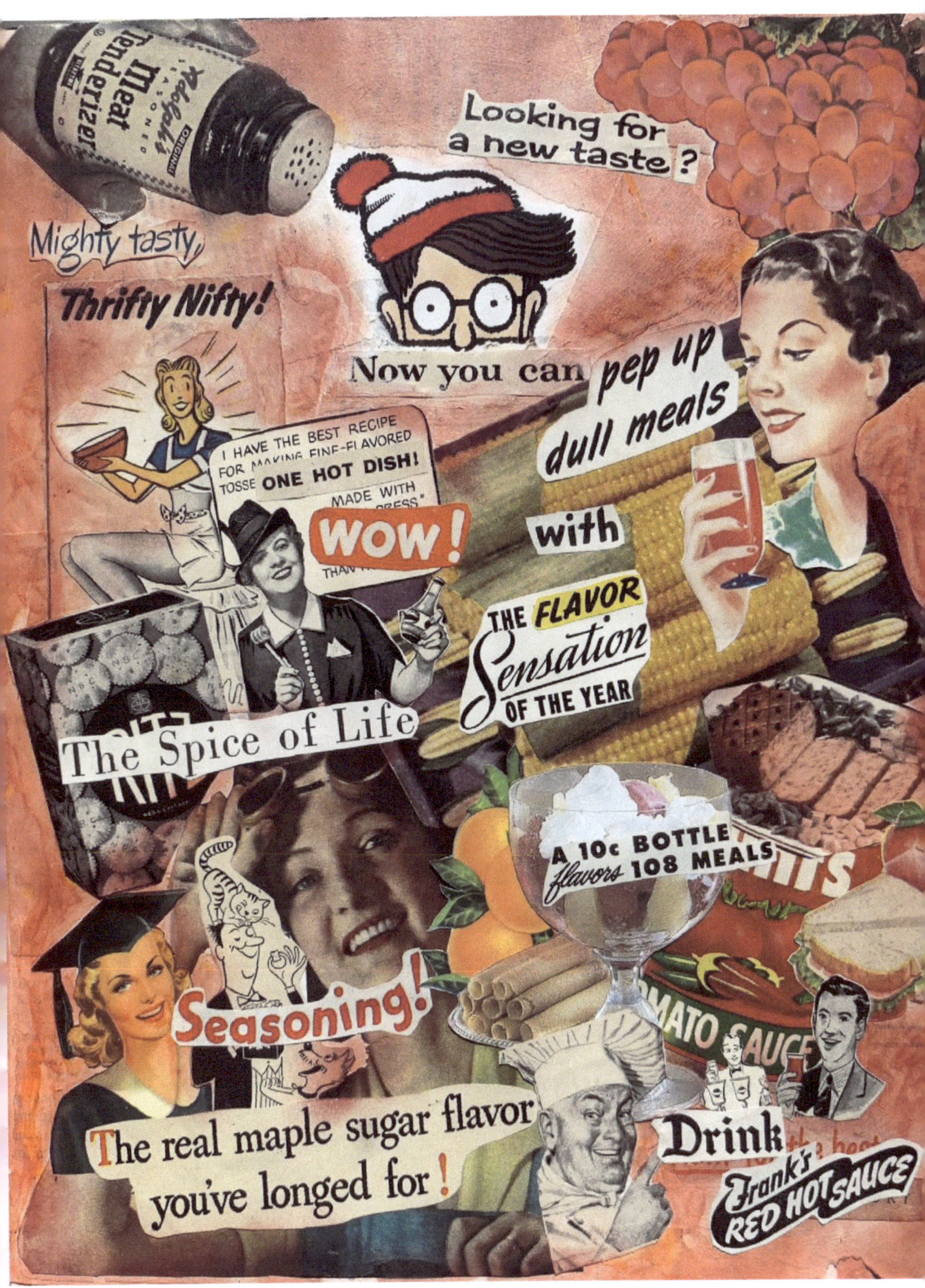
Adolph's
Meat Tenderizer
Looking for a new taste?
Mighty tasty,
Thrifty Nifty!
Now you can pep up dull meals
I HAVE THE BEST RECIPE FOR MAKING FINE-FLAVORED
ONE HOT DISH!
MADE WITH
WOW!
with
THE FLAVOR Sensation OF THE YEAR
The Spice of Life
A 10c BOTTLE flavors 108 MEALS
Seasoning!
The real maple sugar flavor you've longed for!
Drink
Frank's RED HOT SAUCE

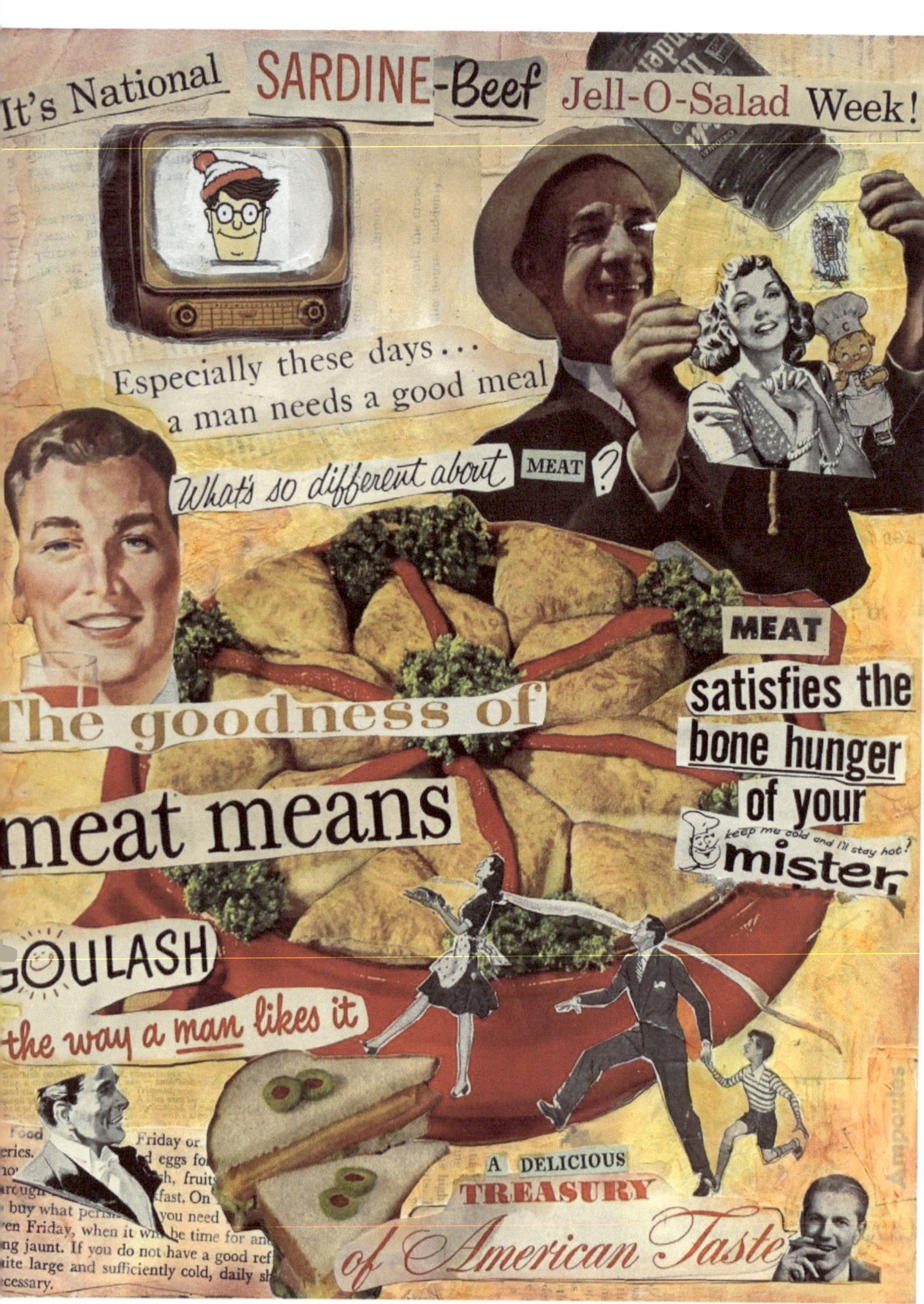
It's National SARDINE-Beef Jell-O-Salad Week!
Especially these days . . .
a man needs a good meal
What's so different about MEAT ?
MEAT
satisfies the
bone hunger
of your
keep me cold and I'll stay hot
mister
The goodness of
meat means
GOULASH
the way a man likes it
A DELICIOUS
TREASURY
of American Taste

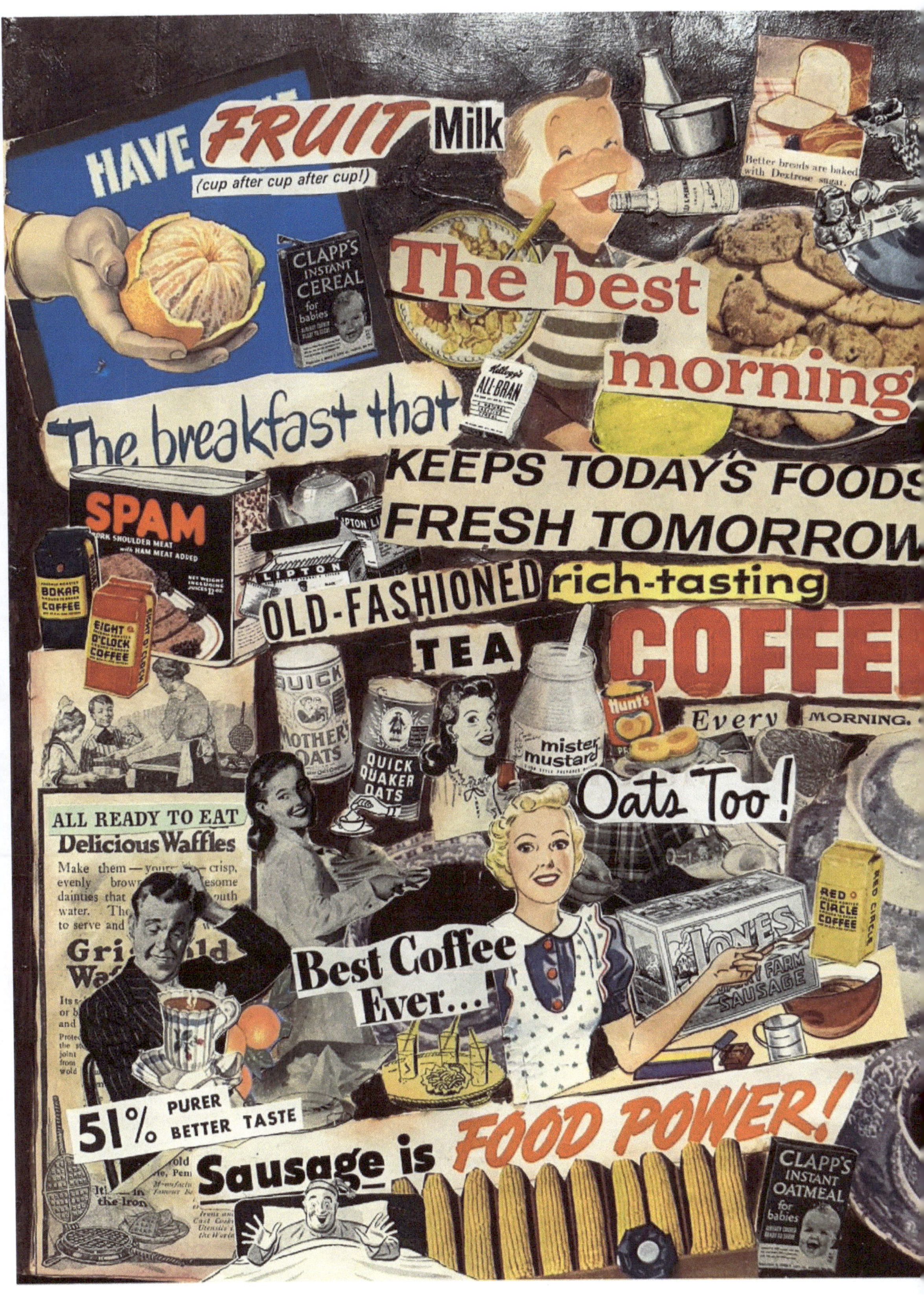
HAVE FRUIT Milk
(cup after cup after cup!)
CLAPP'S INSTANT CEREAL for babies
The best morning
Better breads are baked with Dextrose sugar.
The breakfast that
ALL-BRAN
KEEPS TODAY'S FOODS
FRESH TOMORROW
SPAM
BOKAR COFFEE
EIGHT O'CLOCK COFFEE
LIPTON
OLD-FASHIONED rich-tasting
TEA
COFFE
Every MORNING.
QUICK MOTHER'S OATS
QUICK QUAKER OATS
mister mustard
Hunt's
Oats Too!
ALL READY TO EAT
Delicious Waffles
RED CIRCLE COFFEE
JONES FARM SAUSAGE
Best Coffee Ever...
51% PURER BETTER TASTE
Sausage is FOOD POWER!
CLAPP'S INSTANT OATMEAL for babies

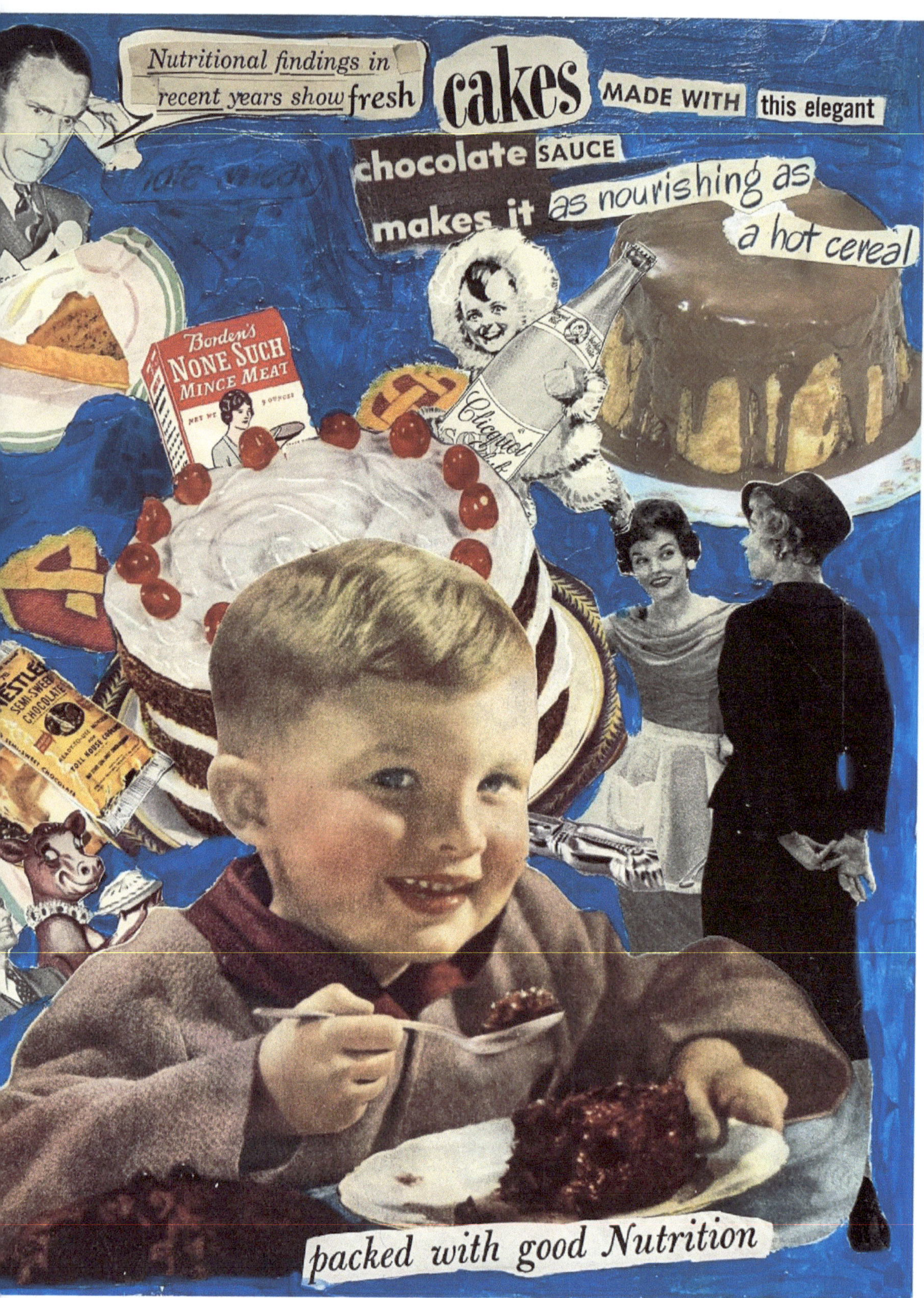
Nutritional findings in recent years show fresh
cakes
MADE WITH
this elegant
chocolate SAUCE
makes it
as nourishing as
a hot cereal
Borden's
NONE SUCH
MINCE MEAT
packed with good Nutrition

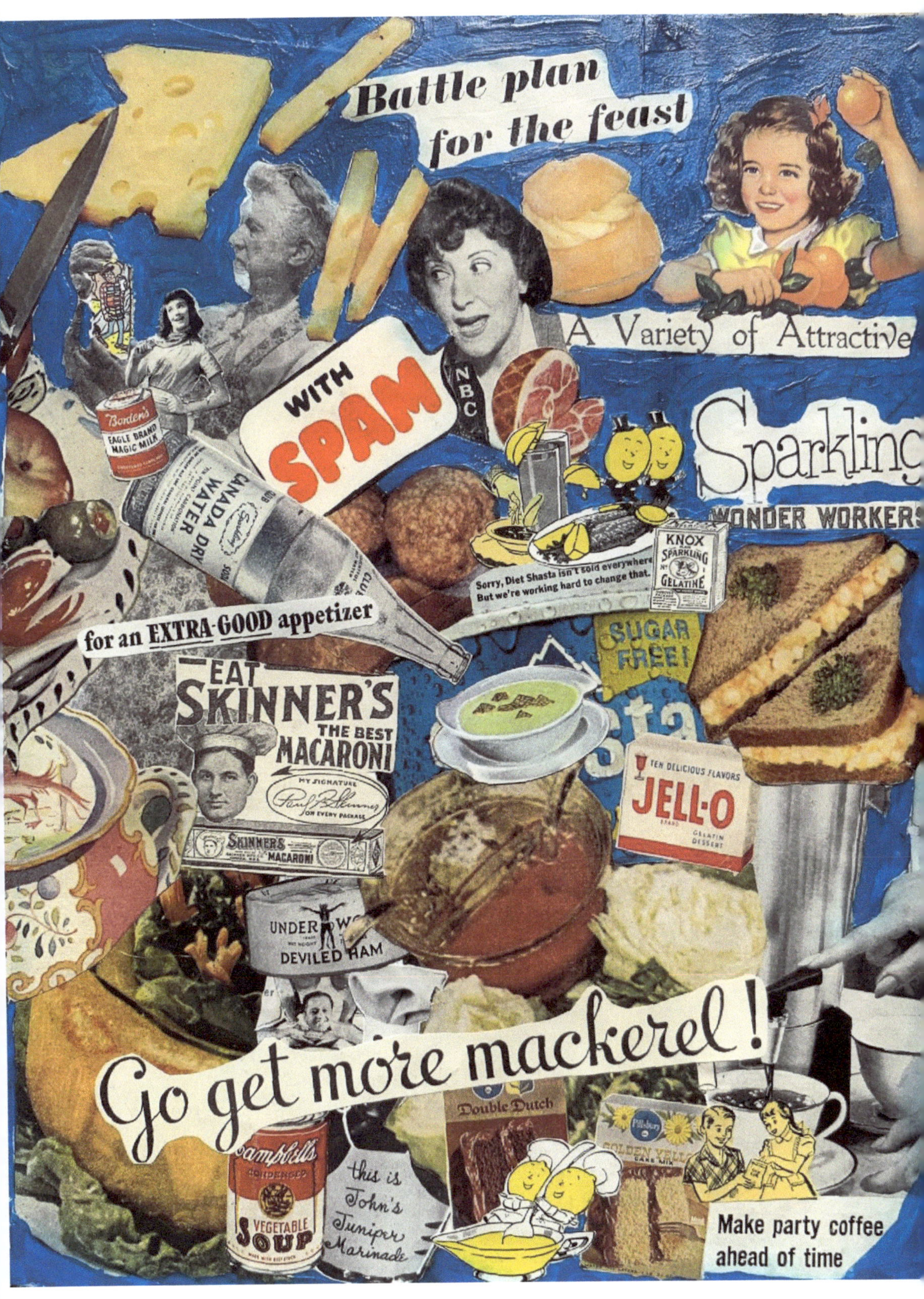
Battle plan for the feast
A Variety of Attractive
WITH SPAM
Sparkling
WONDER WORKERS
KNOX SPARKLING GELATINE
Sorry, Diet Shasta isn't sold everywhere. But we're working hard to change that.
SUGAR FREE!
for an EXTRA-GOOD appetizer
EAT SKINNER'S THE BEST MACARONI
MY SIGNATURE ON EVERY PACKAGE
SKINNERS MACARONI
TEN DELICIOUS FLAVORS
JELL-O
GELATIN DESSERT
UNDERWOOD DEVILED HAM
Go get more mackerel!
Campbell's VEGETABLE SOUP
this is John's Juniper Marinade
Double Dutch
Make party coffee ahead of time
Borden's EAGLE BRAND MAGIC MILK
CANADA DRY WATER

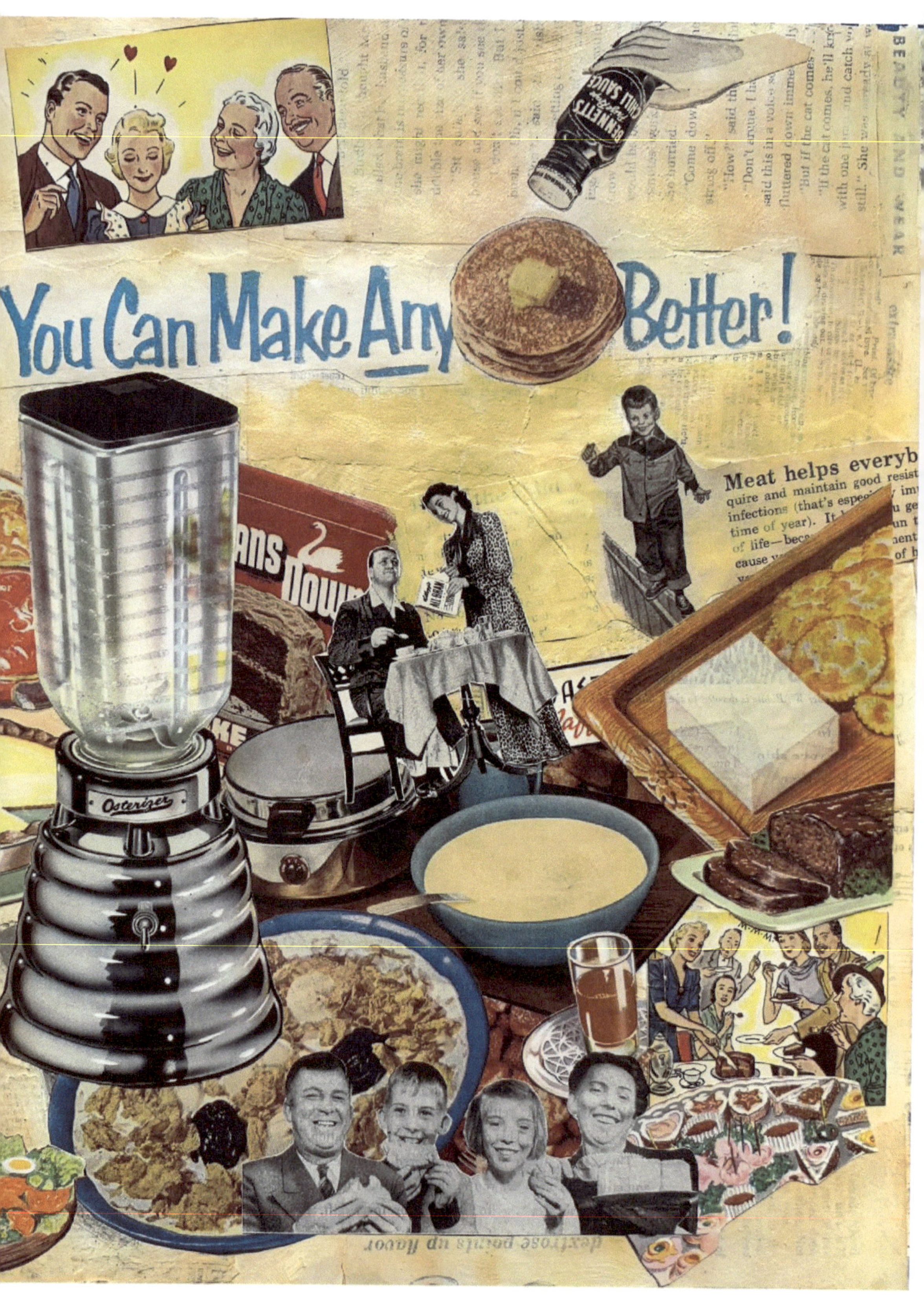
You Can Make Any Better!
BENNETT'S CHILI SAUCE
Meat helps everyb
Osterizer
dextrose points up flavor

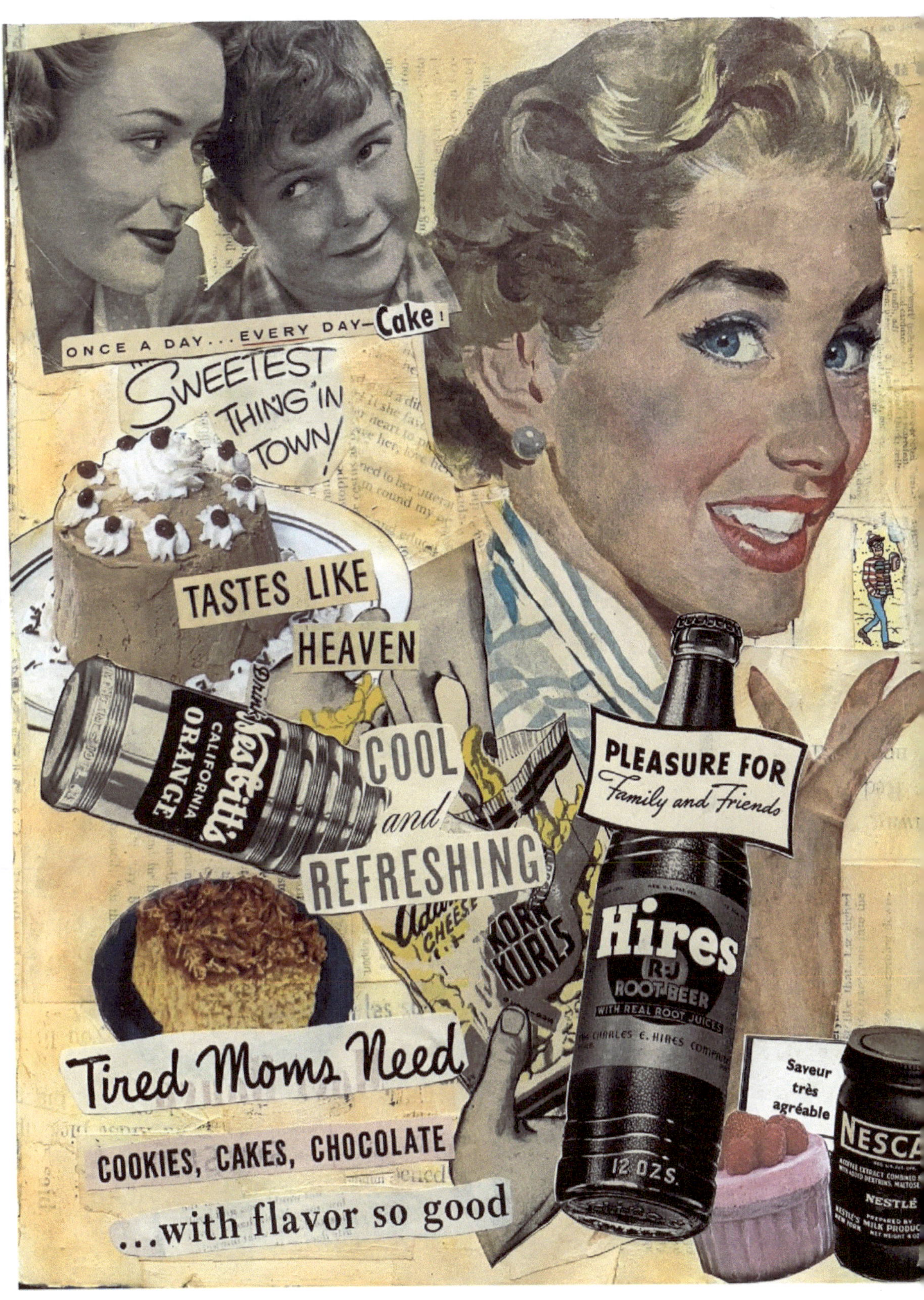
ONCE A DAY... EVERY DAY—Cake!
SWEETEST THING IN TOWN!
TASTES LIKE
HEAVEN
Drink Nesbitt's CALIFORNIA ORANGE
COOL
and
REFRESHING
PLEASURE FOR
Family and Friends
KORN KURLS
Hires
R-J
ROOT BEER
WITH REAL ROOT JUICES
12 OZS.
Saveur
très
agréable
NESCA
NESTLÉ
Tired Moms Need
COOKIES, CAKES, CHOCOLATE
...with flavor so good

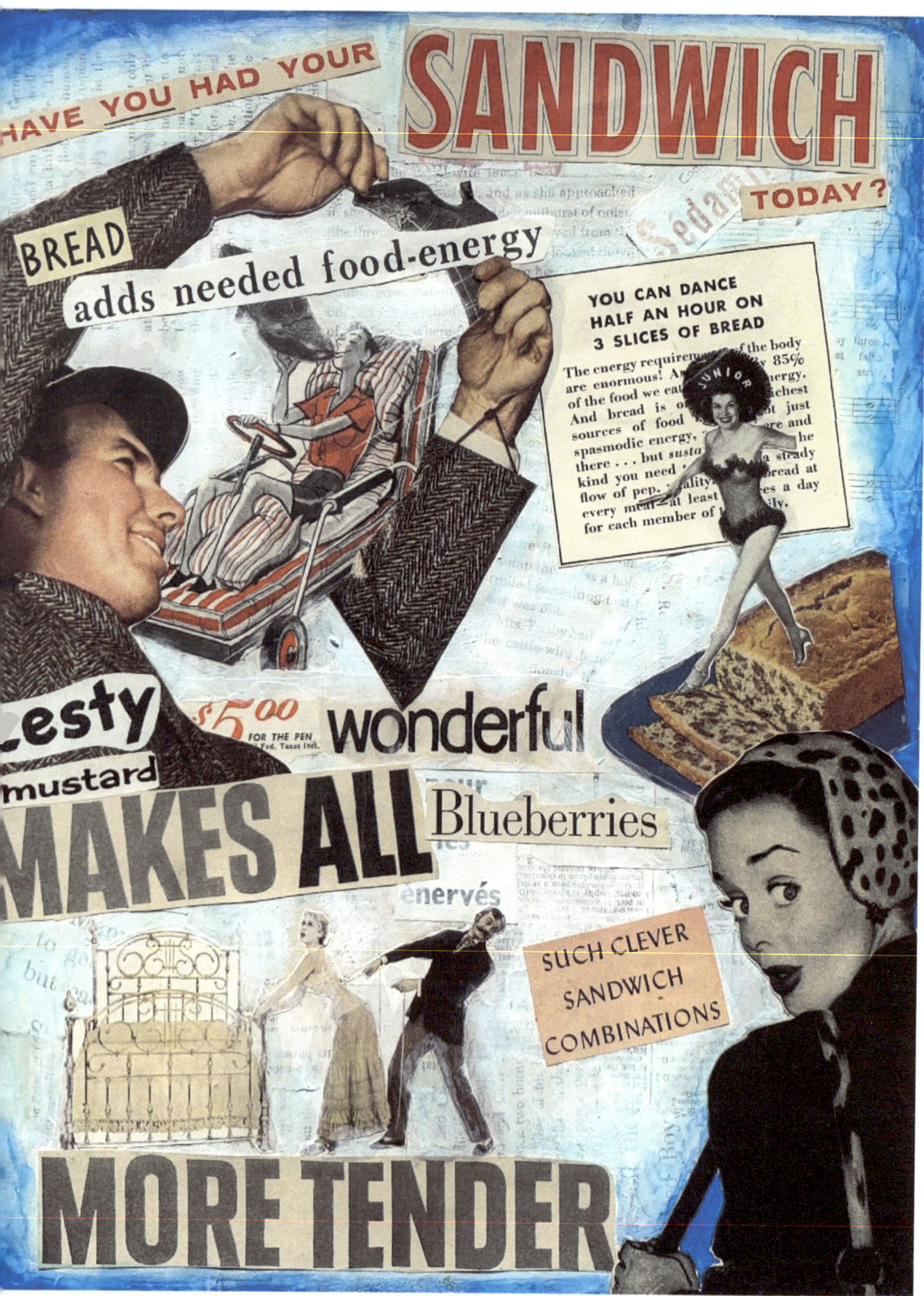
HAVE YOU HAD YOUR
SANDWICH
TODAY?
BREAD
adds needed food-energy
YOU CAN DANCE
HALF AN HOUR ON
3 SLICES OF BREAD
JUNIOR
esty
$5.00 FOR THE PEN
wonderful
mustard
MAKES ALL
Blueberries
enervés
SUCH CLEVER
SANDWICH
COMBINATIONS
MORE TENDER

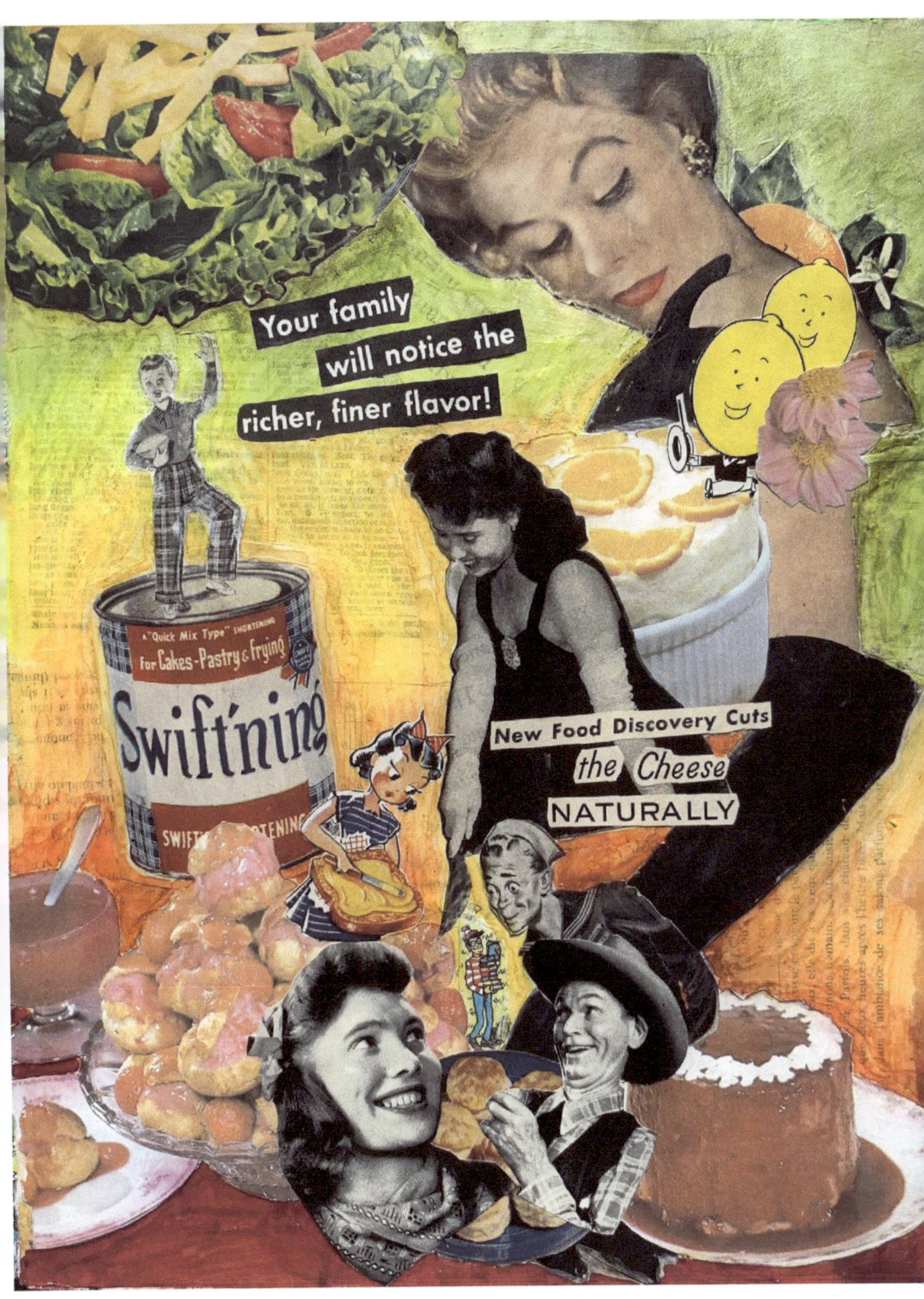
Your family
will notice the
richer, finer flavor!
A "Quick Mix Type" SHORTENING
For Cakes-Pastry & Frying
Swift'ning
New Food Discovery Cuts
the Cheese
NATURALLY

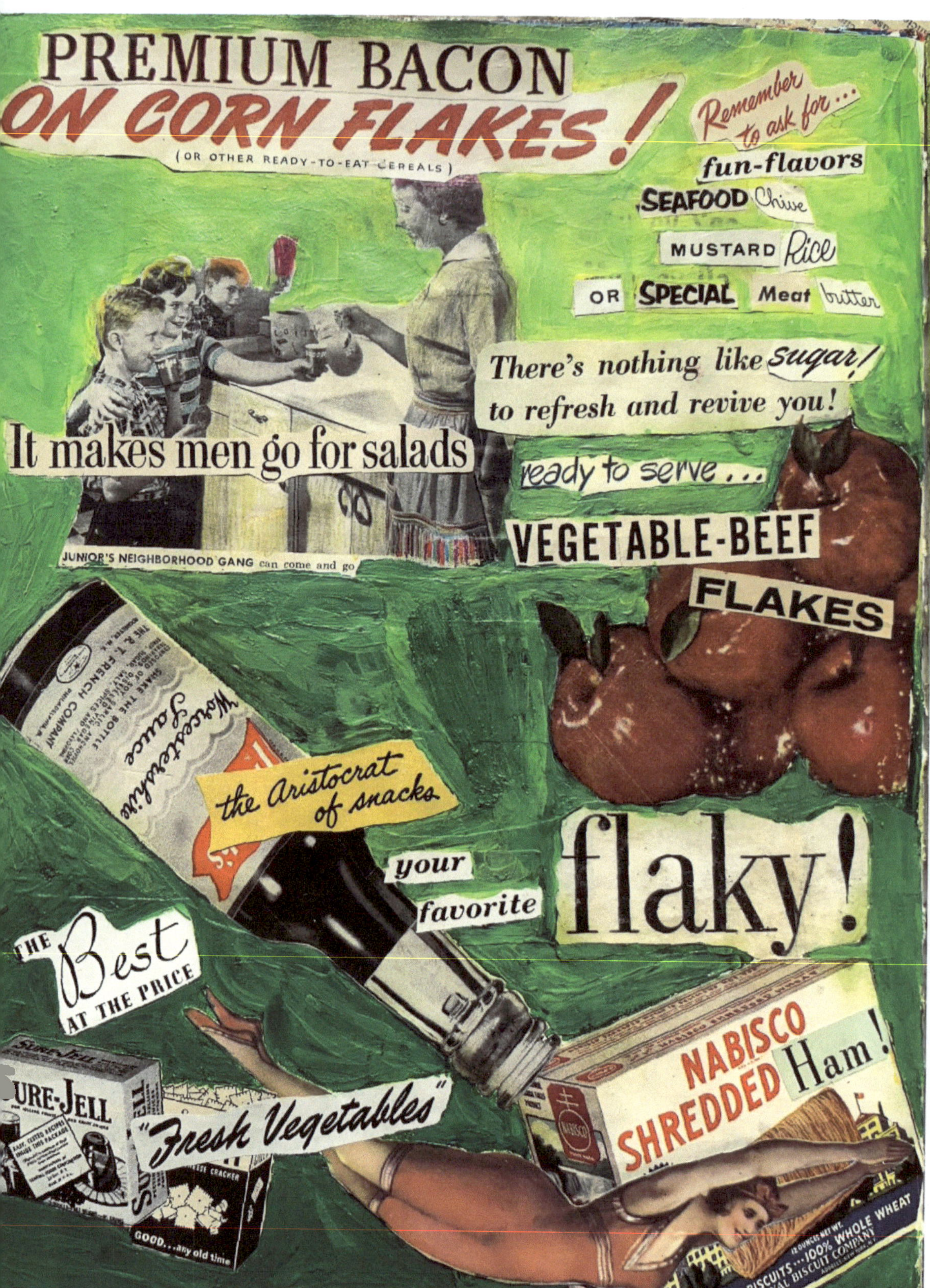
PREMIUM BACON
ON CORN FLAKES!
(OR OTHER READY-TO-EAT CEREALS)
Remember to ask for...
fun-flavors
SEAFOOD Chive
MUSTARD Rice
OR SPECIAL Meat butter
There's nothing like sugar!
to refresh and revive you!
It makes men go for salads
ready to serve...
VEGETABLE-BEEF
FLAKES
JUNIOR'S NEIGHBORHOOD GANG can come and go
Worcestershire Sauce
the Aristocrat of snacks
your
favorite
flaky!
THE Best AT THE PRICE
SURE-JELL
"Fresh Vegetables"
GOOD...any old time
NABISCO SHREDDED Ham!
BISCUITS...100% WHOLE WHEAT

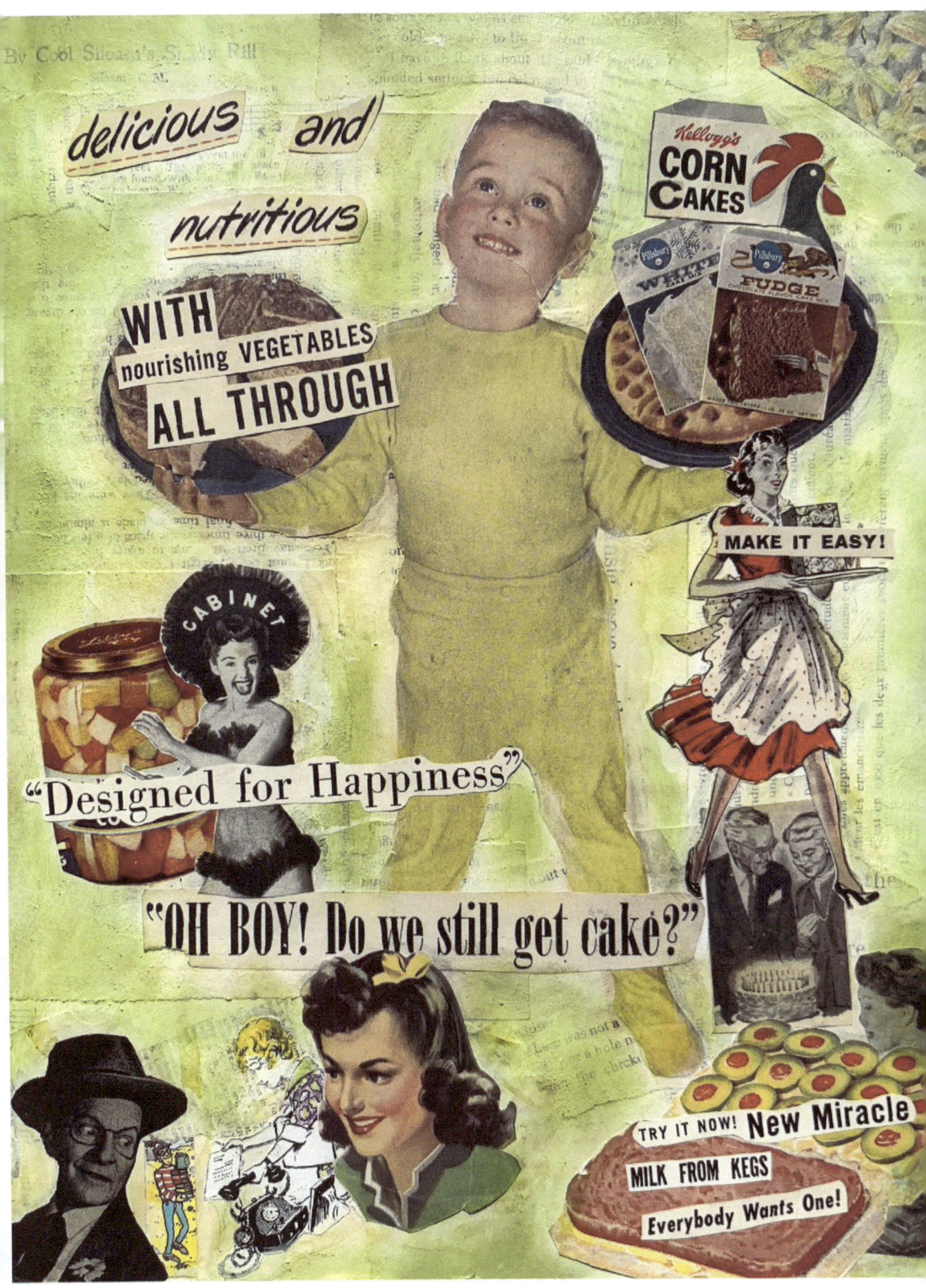

delicious and
nutritious
WITH
nourishing VEGETABLES
ALL THROUGH
Kellogg's
CORN
CAKES
WHITE
FUDGE
MAKE IT EASY!
CABINET
"Designed for Happiness"
"OH BOY! Do we still get cake?"
TRY IT NOW! New Miracle
MILK FROM KEGS
Everybody Wants One!

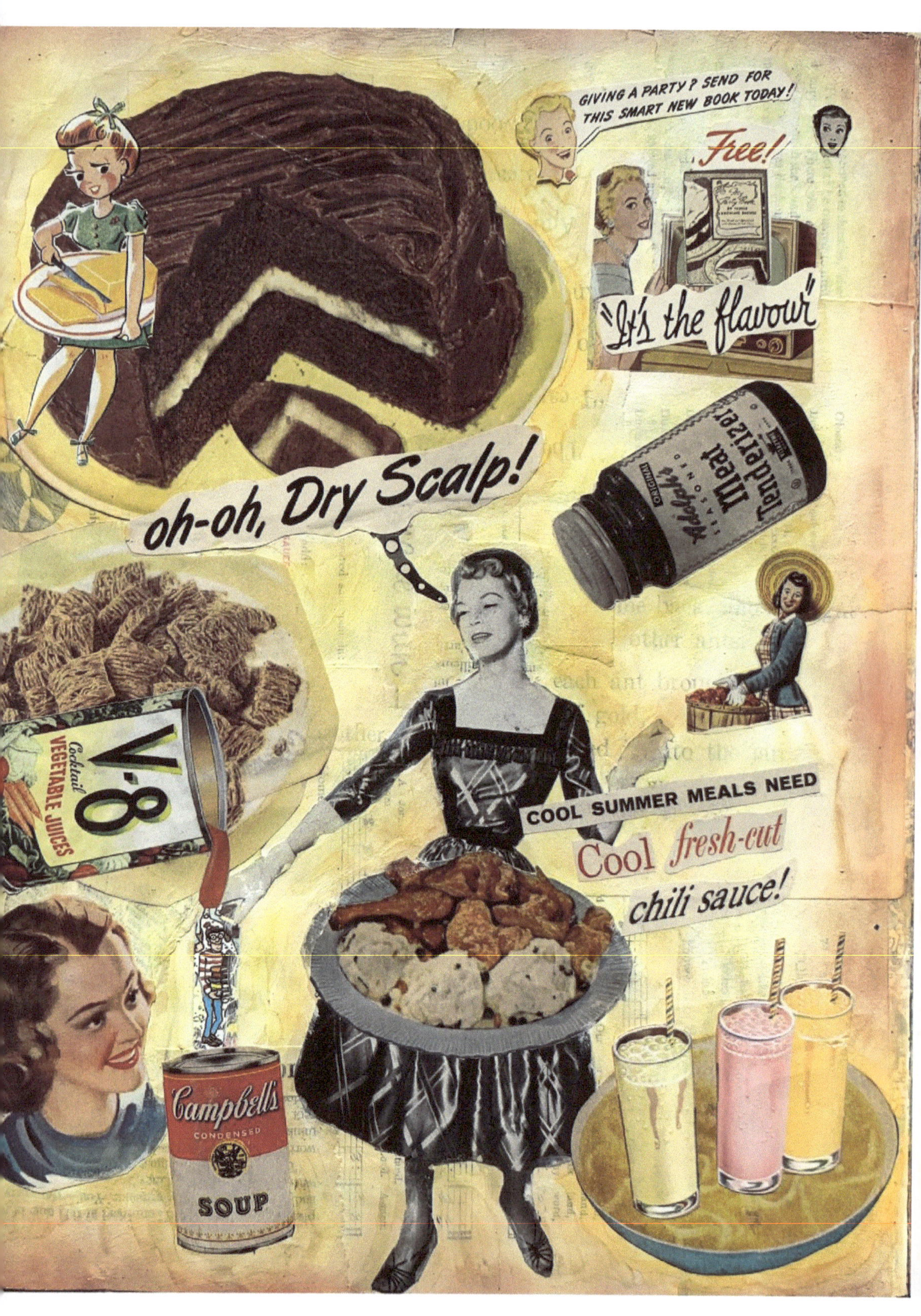
GIVING A PARTY? SEND FOR THIS SMART NEW BOOK TODAY!
Free!
"It's the flavour"
Adolph's ORIGINAL SEASONED Meat Tenderizer
oh-oh, Dry Scalp!
V-8 Cocktail VEGETABLE JUICES
COOL SUMMER MEALS NEED
Cool fresh-cut
chili sauce!
Campbell's CONDENSED
SOUP

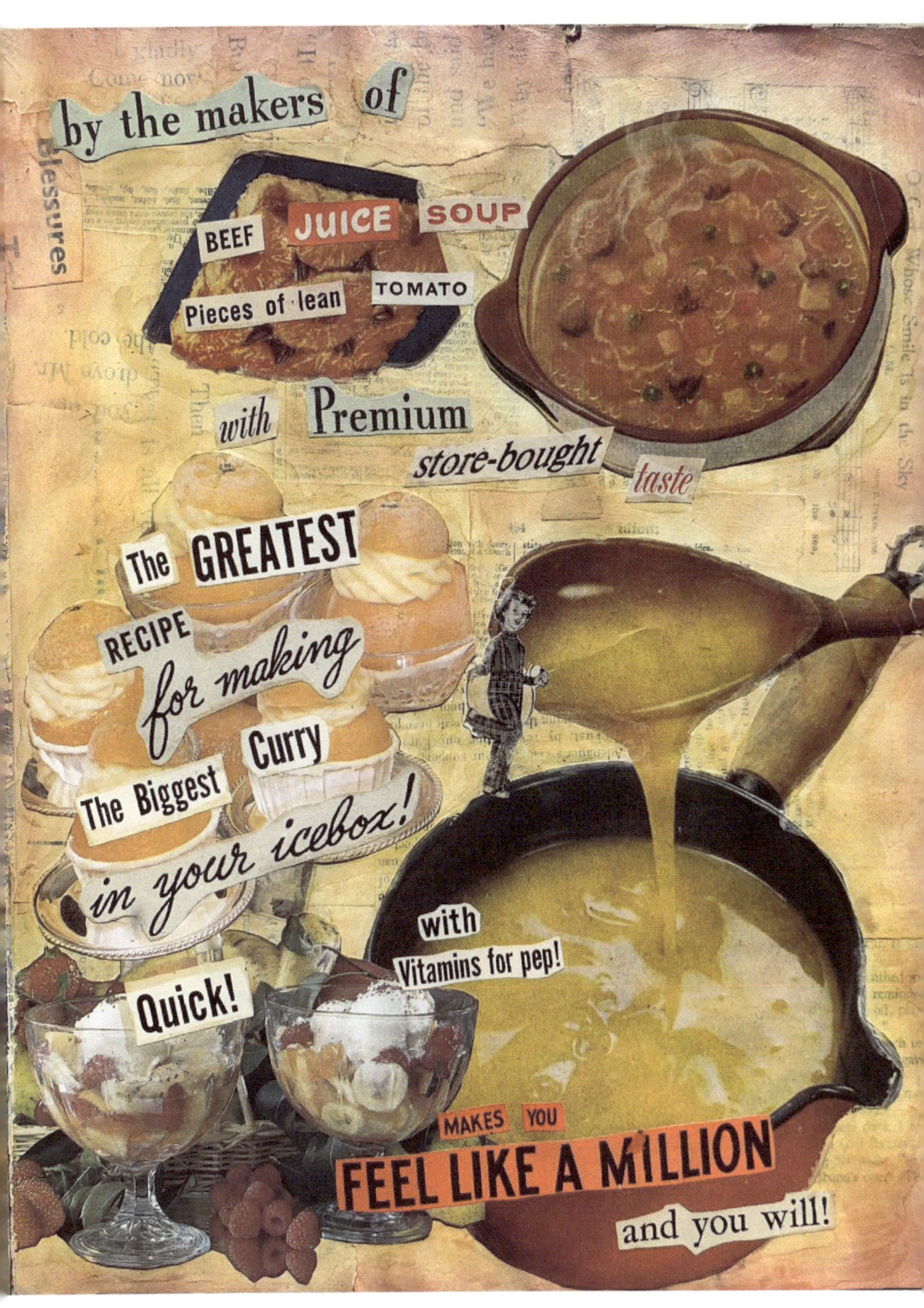
by the makers of
BEEF
JUICE
SOUP
Pieces of lean
TOMATO
with
Premium
store-bought
taste
The GREATEST
RECIPE
for making
The Biggest
Curry
in your icebox!
with
Vitamins for pep!
Quick!
MAKES YOU
FEEL LIKE A MILLION
and you will!

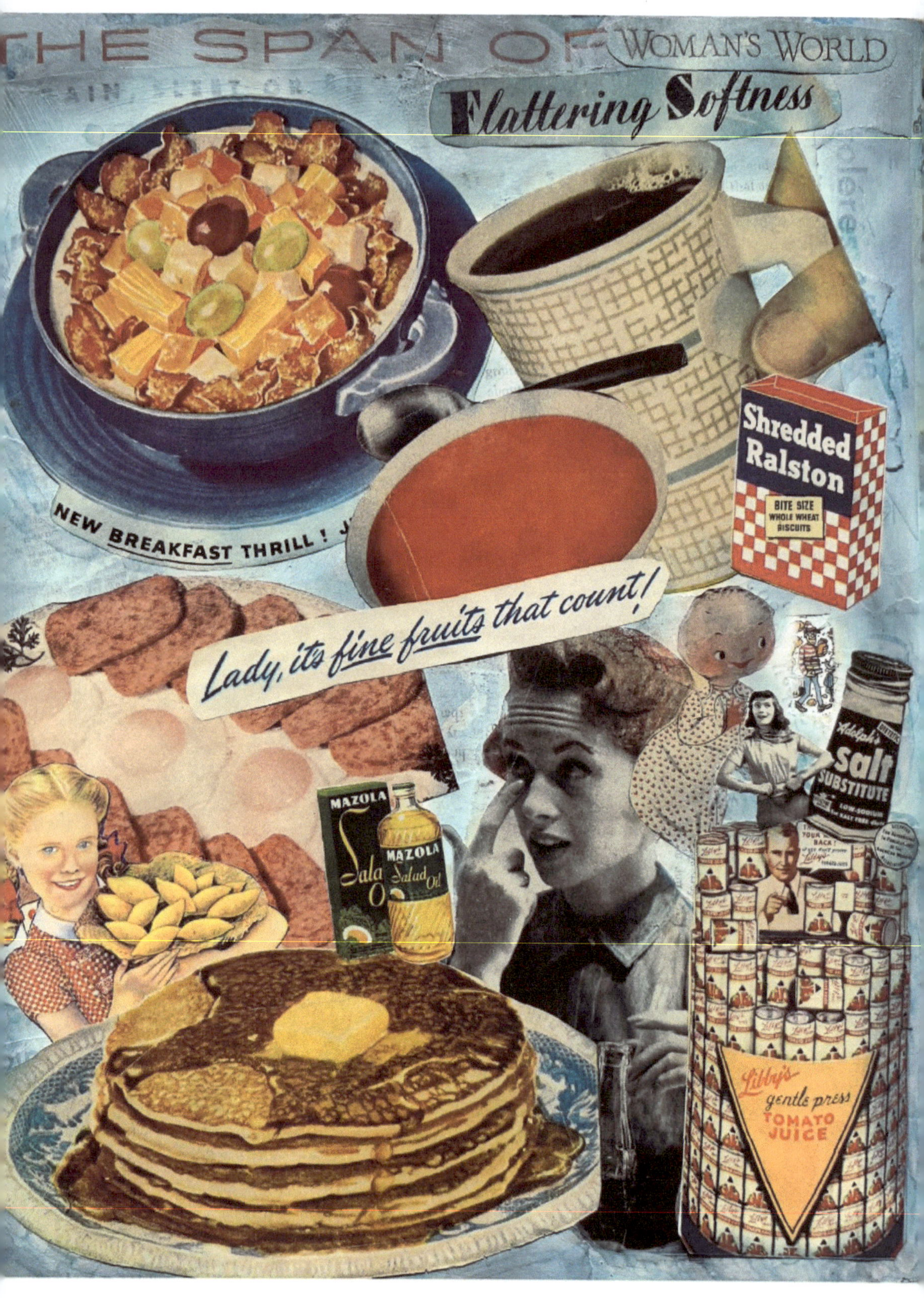
THE SPAN OF WOMAN'S WORLD
Flattering Softness
NEW BREAKFAST THRILL !
Shredded Ralston
BITE SIZE WHOLE WHEAT BISCUITS
Lady, it's fine fruits that count!
MAZOLA
MAZOLA Salad Oil
Adolph's salt SUBSTITUTE
Libby's gentle press TOMATO JUICE

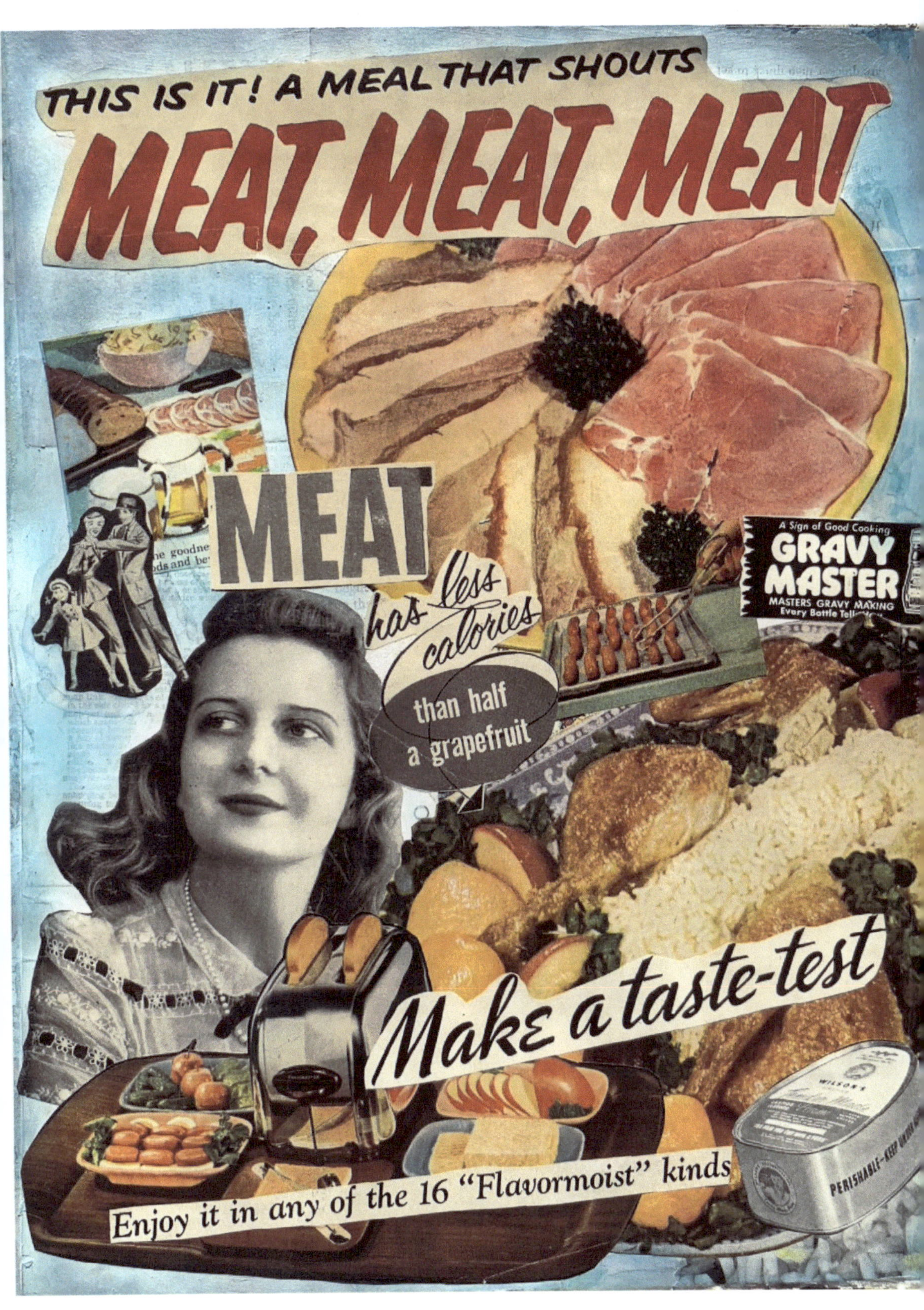
THIS IS IT! A MEAL THAT SHOUTS
MEAT, MEAT, MEAT
MEAT
has less calories
than half a grapefruit
A Sign of Good Cooking
GRAVY MASTER
MASTERS GRAVY MAKING
Make a taste-test
Enjoy it in any of the 16 "Flavormoist" kinds
PERISHABLE

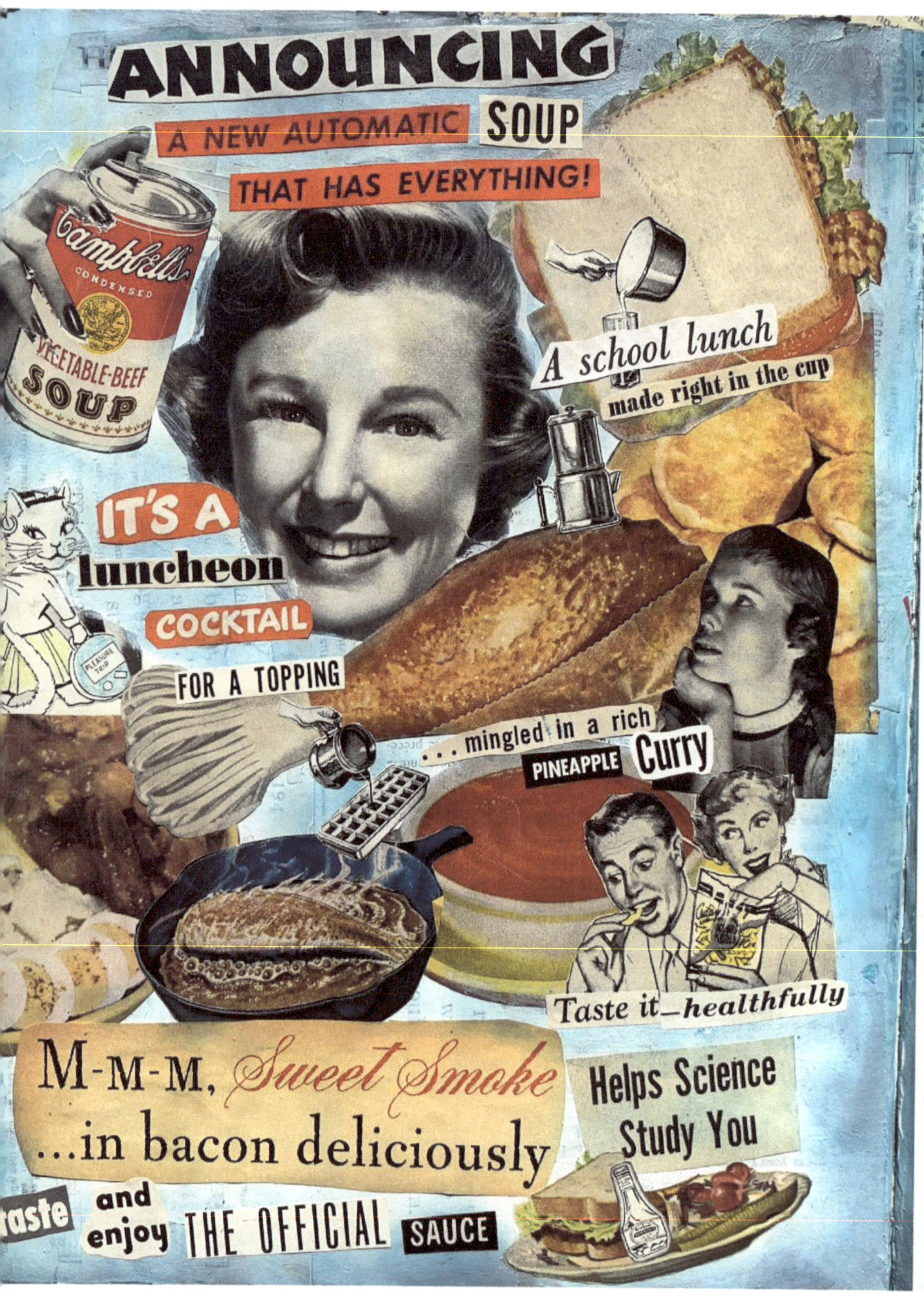
ANNOUNCING
A NEW AUTOMATIC SOUP
THAT HAS EVERYTHING!
Campbell's
CONDENSED
VEGETABLE-BEEF
SOUP
A school lunch
made right in the cup
IT'S A
luncheon
COCKTAIL
PLEASURE TRIP
FOR A TOPPING
... mingled in a rich
PINEAPPLE Curry
Taste it—healthfully
M-M-M, Sweet Smoke
...in bacon deliciously
Helps Science
Study You
taste
and
enjoy THE OFFICIAL SAUCE

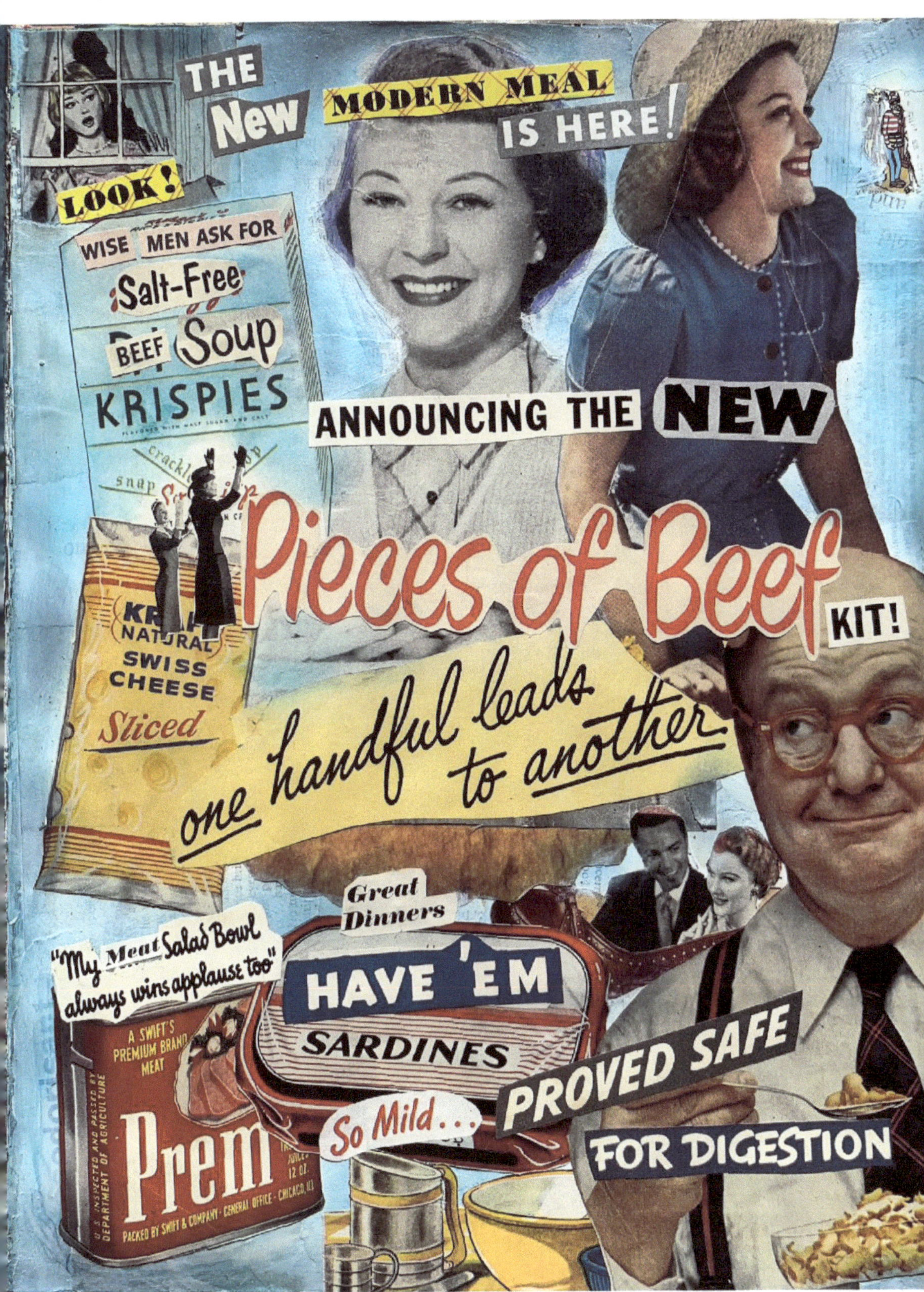
THE New
MODERN MEAL
IS HERE!
LOOK!
WISE MEN ASK FOR
Salt-Free
BEEF Soup
KRISPIES
ANNOUNCING THE NEW
Pieces of Beef
KIT!
NATURAL SWISS CHEESE
Sliced
one handful leads to another
Great Dinners
"My Meat Salad Bowl always wins applause too"
HAVE 'EM
SARDINES
A SWIFT'S PREMIUM BRAND MEAT
Prem
PACKED BY SWIFT & COMPANY · GENERAL OFFICE · CHICAGO, ILL
U. S. INSPECTED AND PASSED BY DEPARTMENT OF AGRICULTURE
So Mild...
PROVED SAFE
FOR DIGESTION

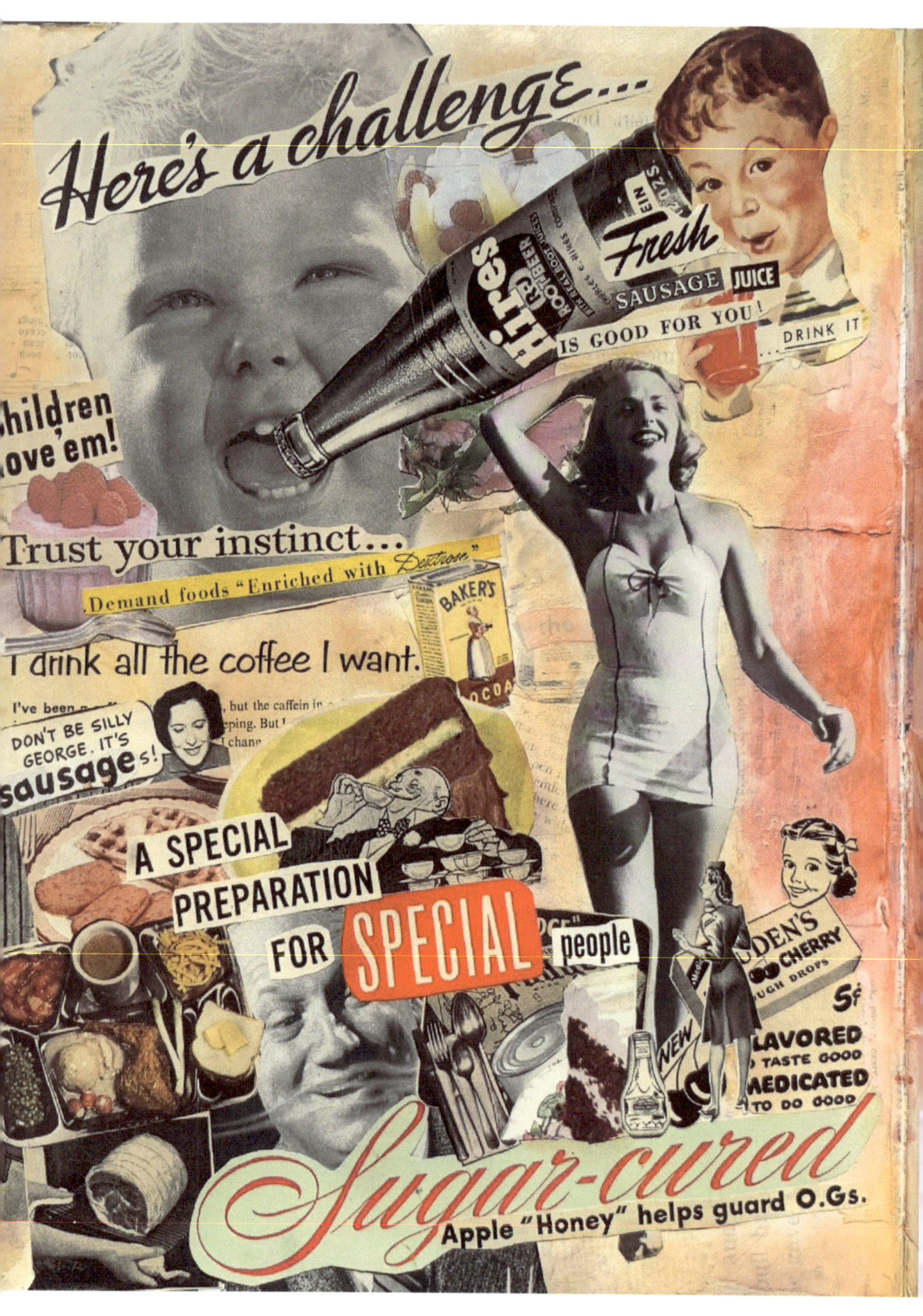
Here's a challenge...
Fresh
SAUSAGE JUICE
IS GOOD FOR YOU!
...DRINK IT
hildren
ove'em!
Trust your instinct...
Demand foods "Enriched with Dextrose"
BAKER'S
COCOA
I drink all the coffee I want.
DON'T BE SILLY GEORGE. IT'S sausages!
A SPECIAL
PREPARATION
FOR SPECIAL people
DEN'S
CHERRY
5¢
NEW
LAVORED
TASTE GOOD
MEDICATED
TO DO GOOD
Sugar-cured
Apple "Honey" helps guard O.G.s.

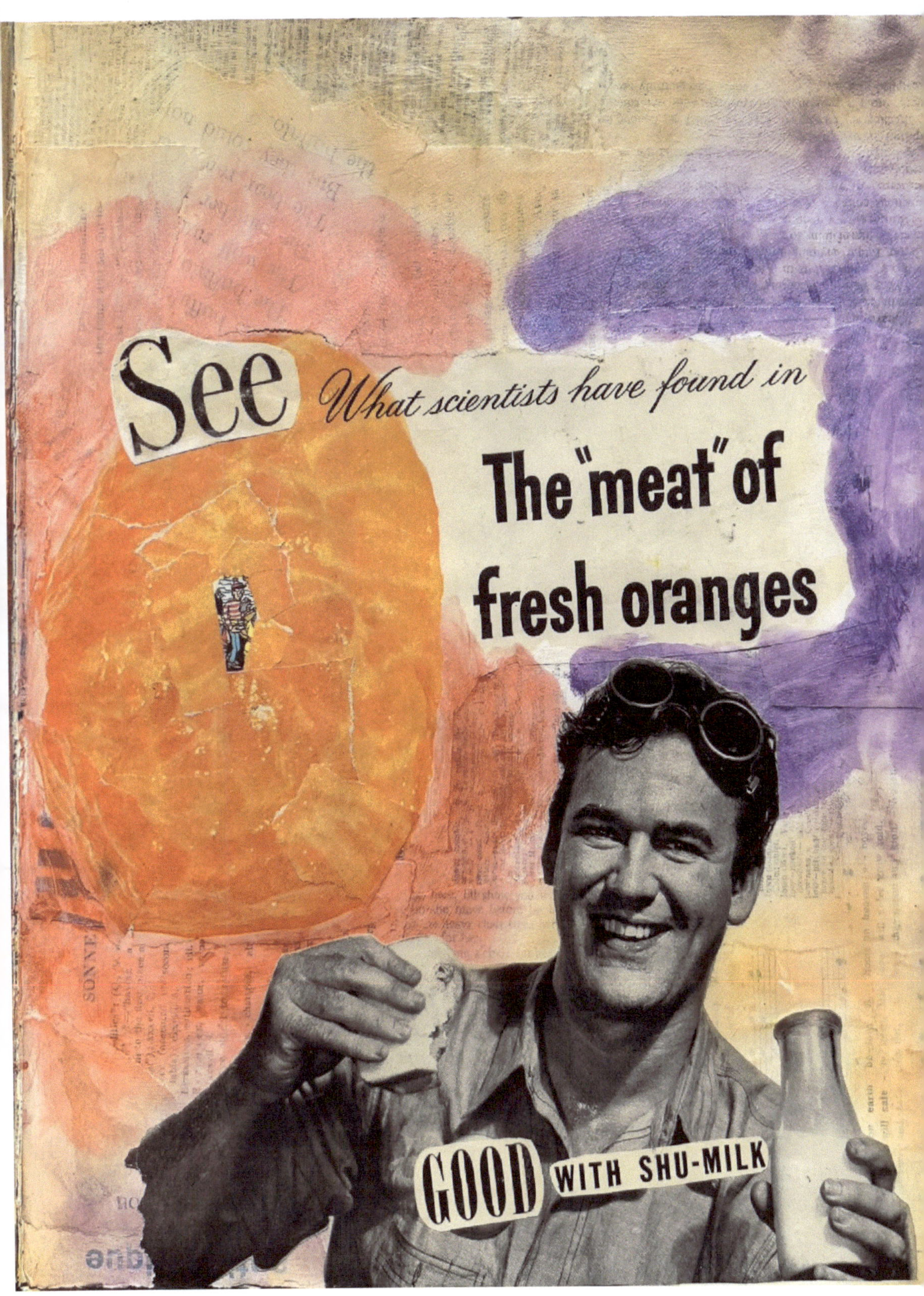
See
What scientists have found in
The "meat" of
fresh oranges
GOOD
WITH SHU-MILK

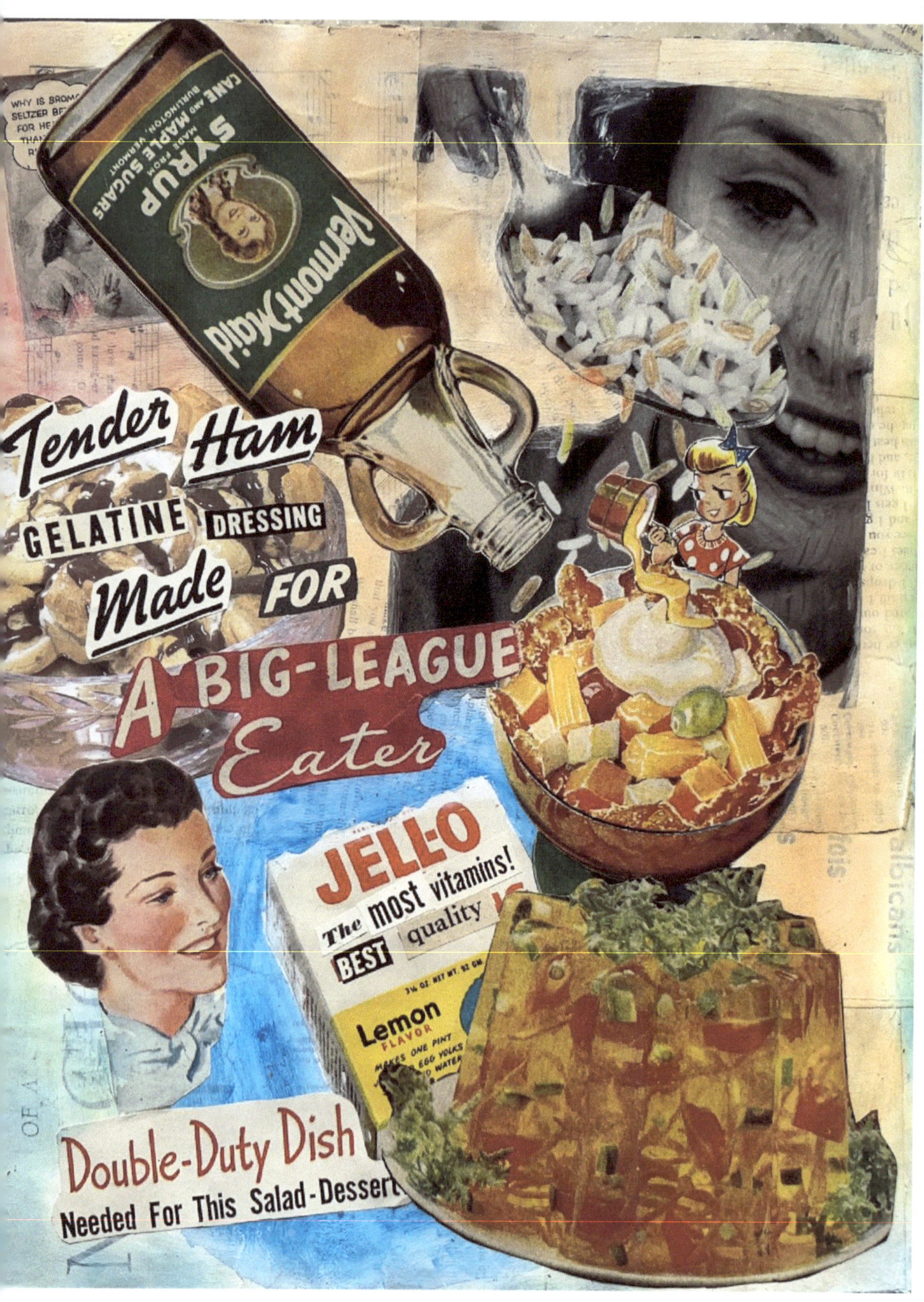

Vermont Maid
SYRUP
MADE FROM CANE AND MAPLE SUGARS
BURLINGTON, VERMONT
Tender Ham
GELATINE DRESSING
Made FOR
A BIG-LEAGUE Eater
JELL-O
The most vitamins!
BEST quality
Lemon FLAVOR
Double-Duty Dish
Needed For This Salad-Dessert

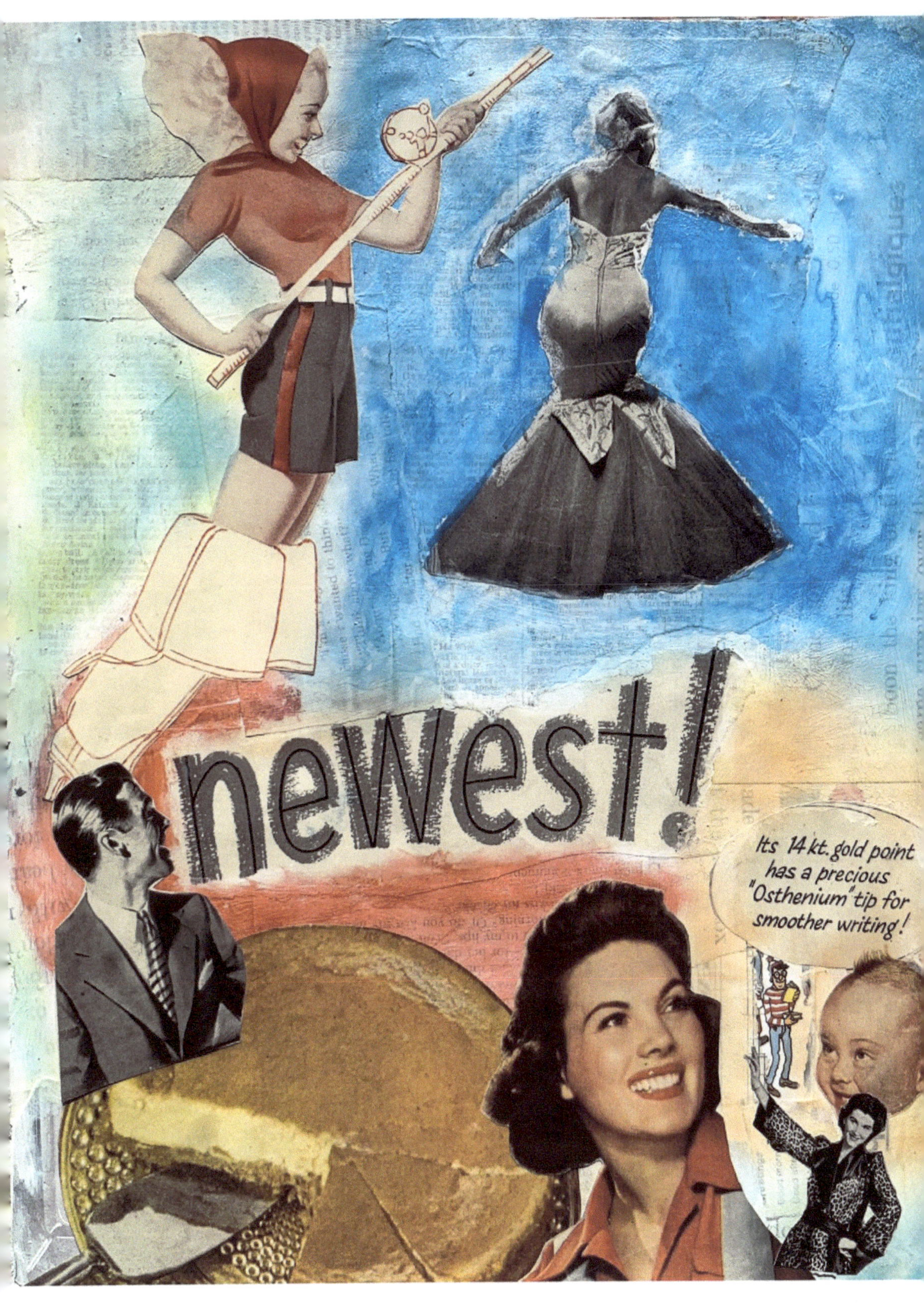
newest!
Its 14 kt. gold point has a precious "Osthenium" tip for smoother writing!

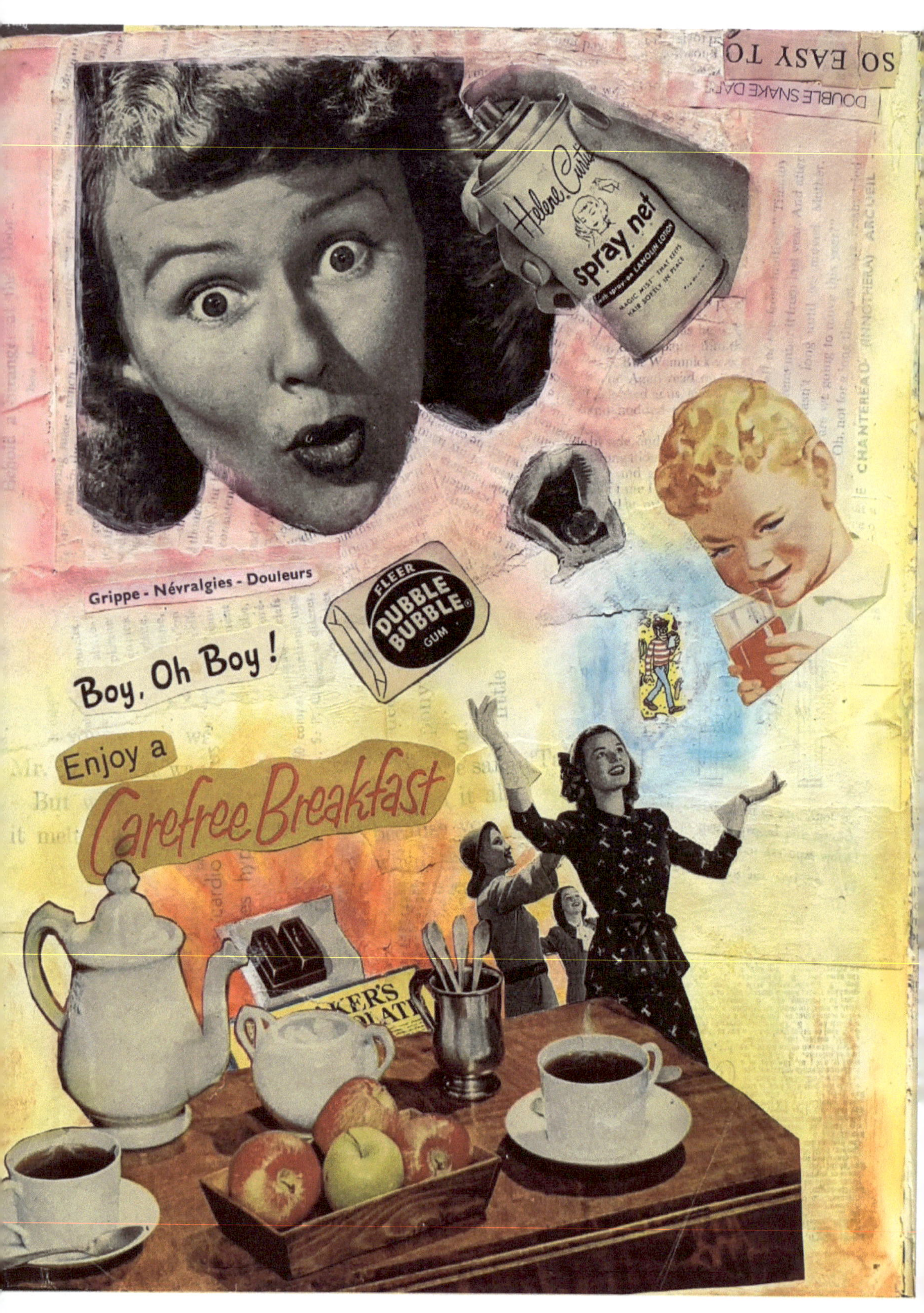
SO EASY TO
DOUBLE SNAKE DAR
Helene Curtis
spray net
Grippe - Névralgies - Douleurs
FLEER
DUBBLE BUBBLE
GUM
Boy, Oh Boy!
Enjoy a
Carefree Breakfast
CHANTEREAU (INNOTHERA) ARCUEIL

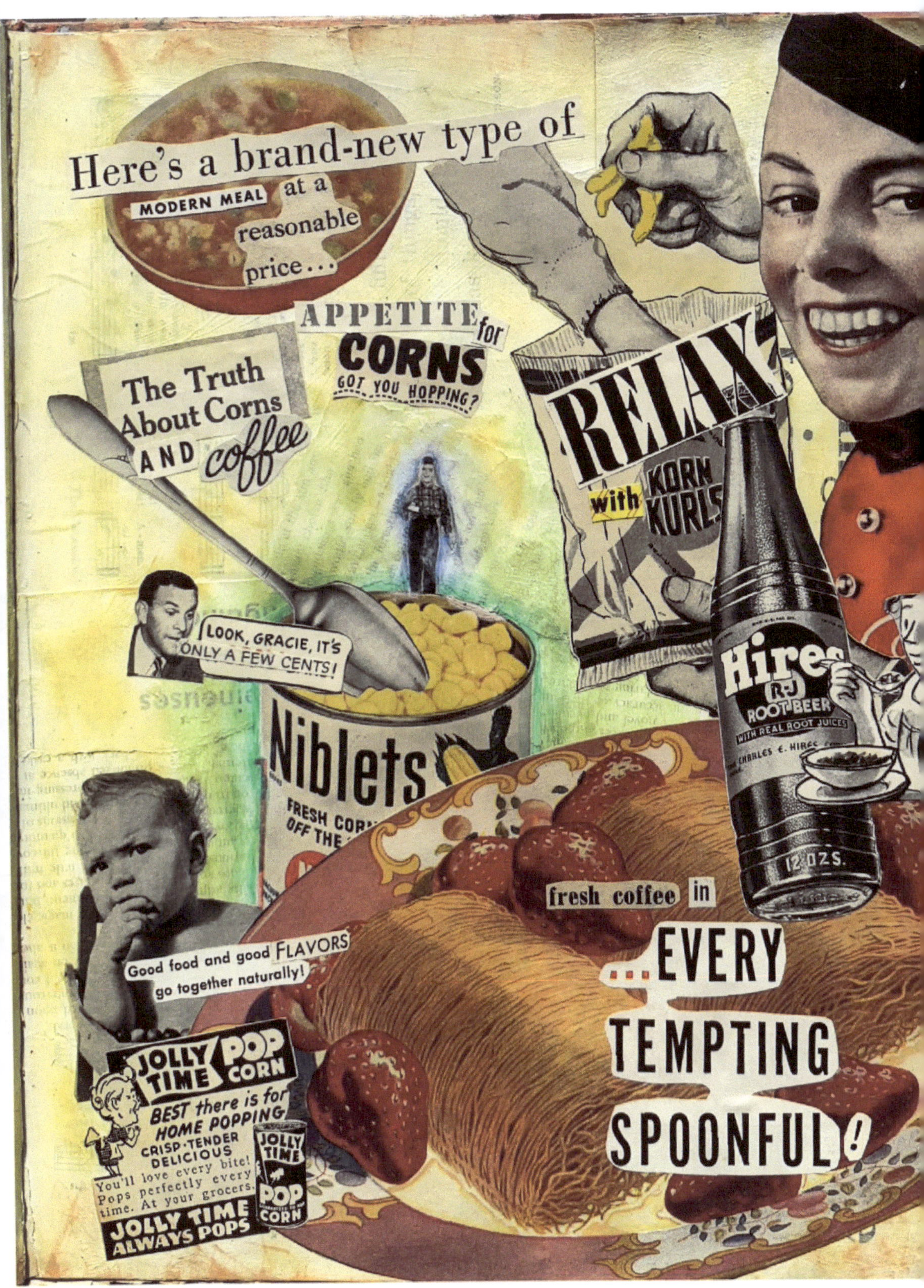
Here's a brand-new type of
MODERN MEAL at a reasonable price...
APPETITE for CORNS GOT YOU HOPPING?
The Truth About Corns AND coffee
RELAX with KORN KURLS
LOOK, GRACIE, IT'S ONLY A FEW CENTS!
Niblets
FRESH CORN OFF THE
Hires R-J ROOT BEER
WITH REAL ROOT JUICES
12 OZS.
fresh coffee in
...EVERY TEMPTING SPOONFUL!
Good food and good FLAVORS go together naturally!
JOLLY TIME POP CORN
BEST there is for HOME POPPING
CRISP-TENDER DELICIOUS
You'll love every bite! Pops perfectly every time. At your grocers.
JOLLY TIME ALWAYS POPS

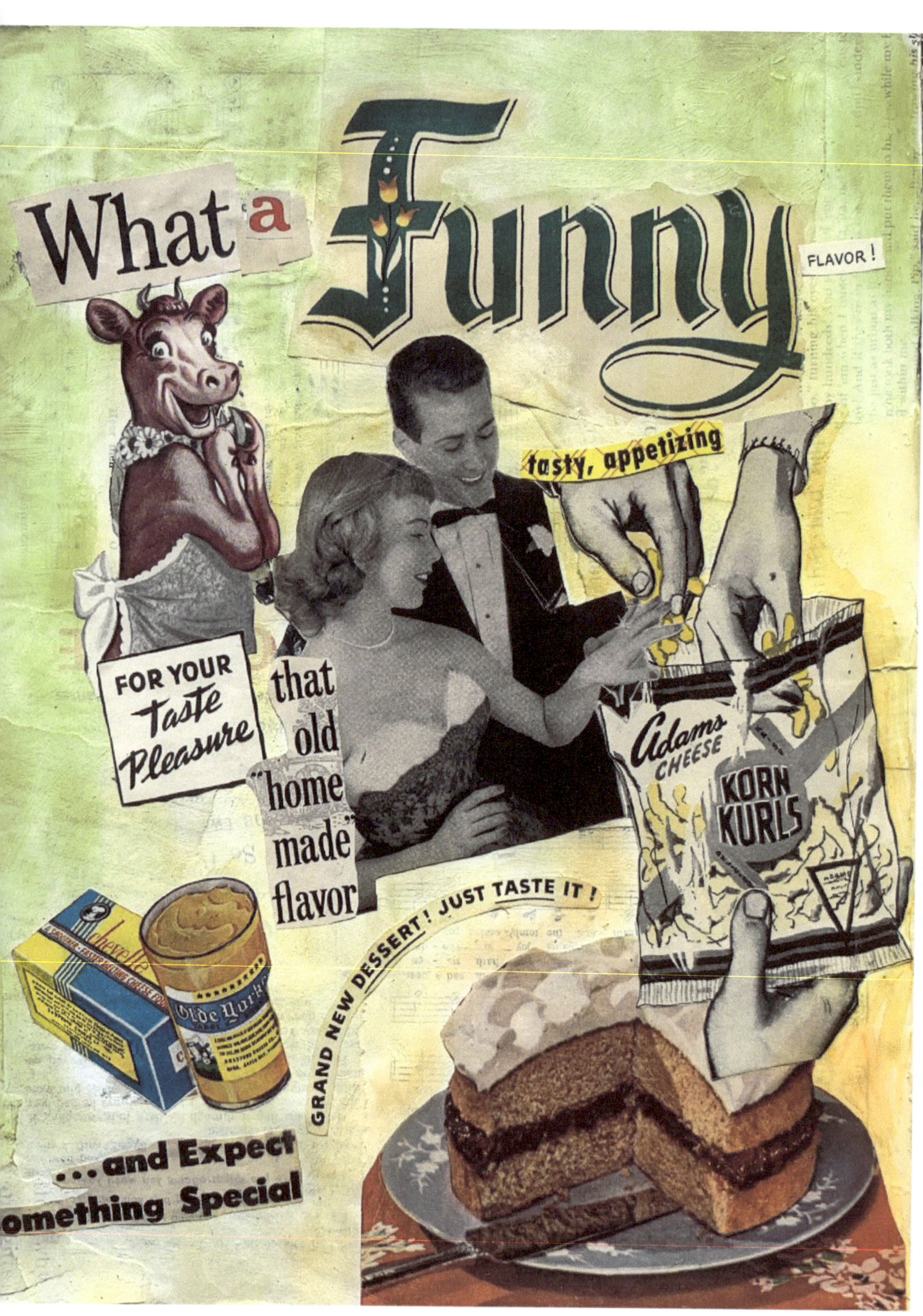
What a Funny
FLAVOR!
tasty, appetizing
FOR YOUR Taste Pleasure
that old "home made" flavor
Adams CHEESE
KORN KURLS
GRAND NEW DESSERT! JUST TASTE IT!
Olde Yorke
...and Expect
omething Special

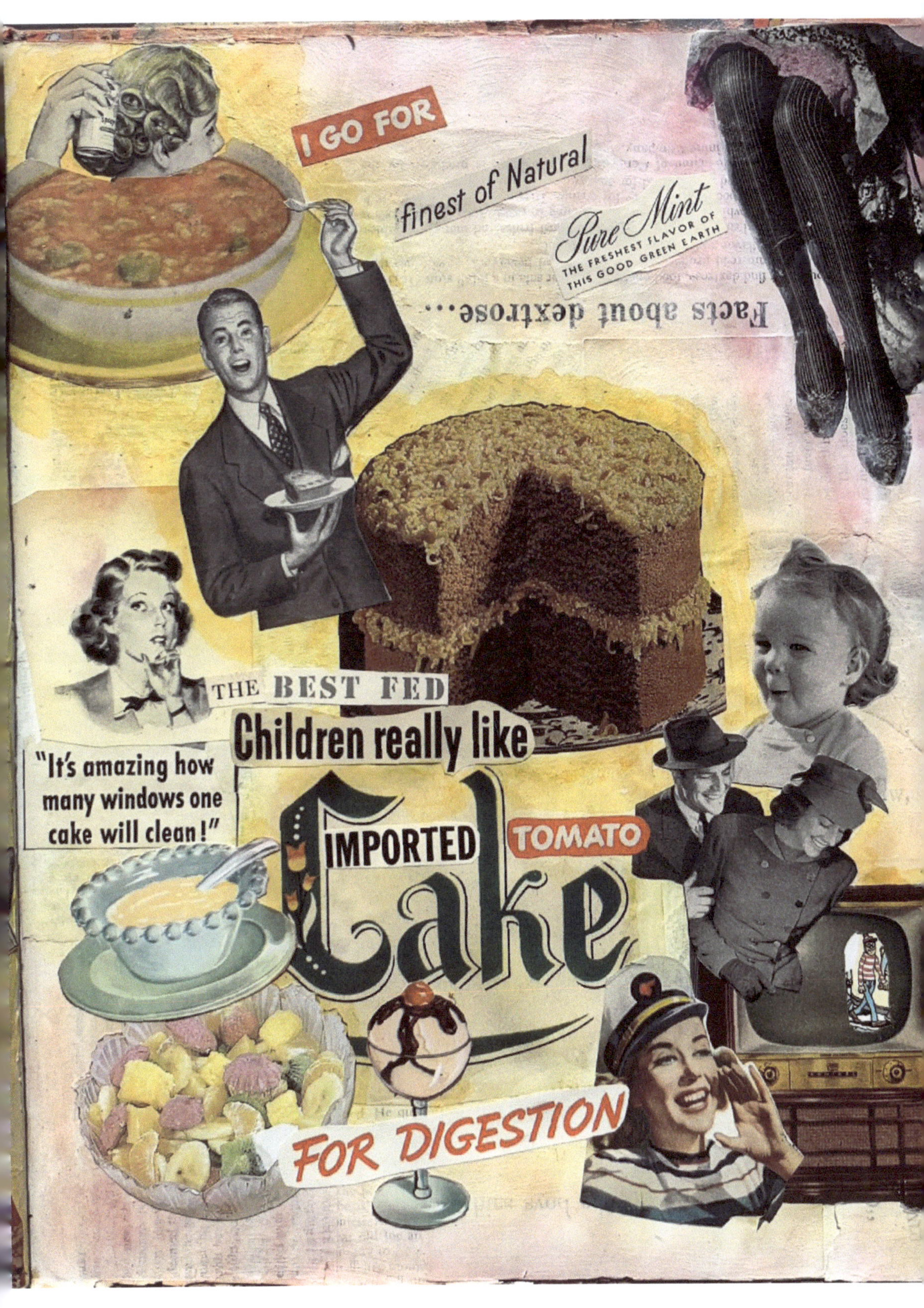
I GO FOR
finest of Natural
Pure Mint
THE FRESHEST FLAVOR OF THIS GOOD GREEN EARTH
Facts about dextrose...
THE BEST FED
Children really like
"It's amazing how many windows one cake will clean!"
IMPORTED
TOMATO
Cake
FOR DIGESTION

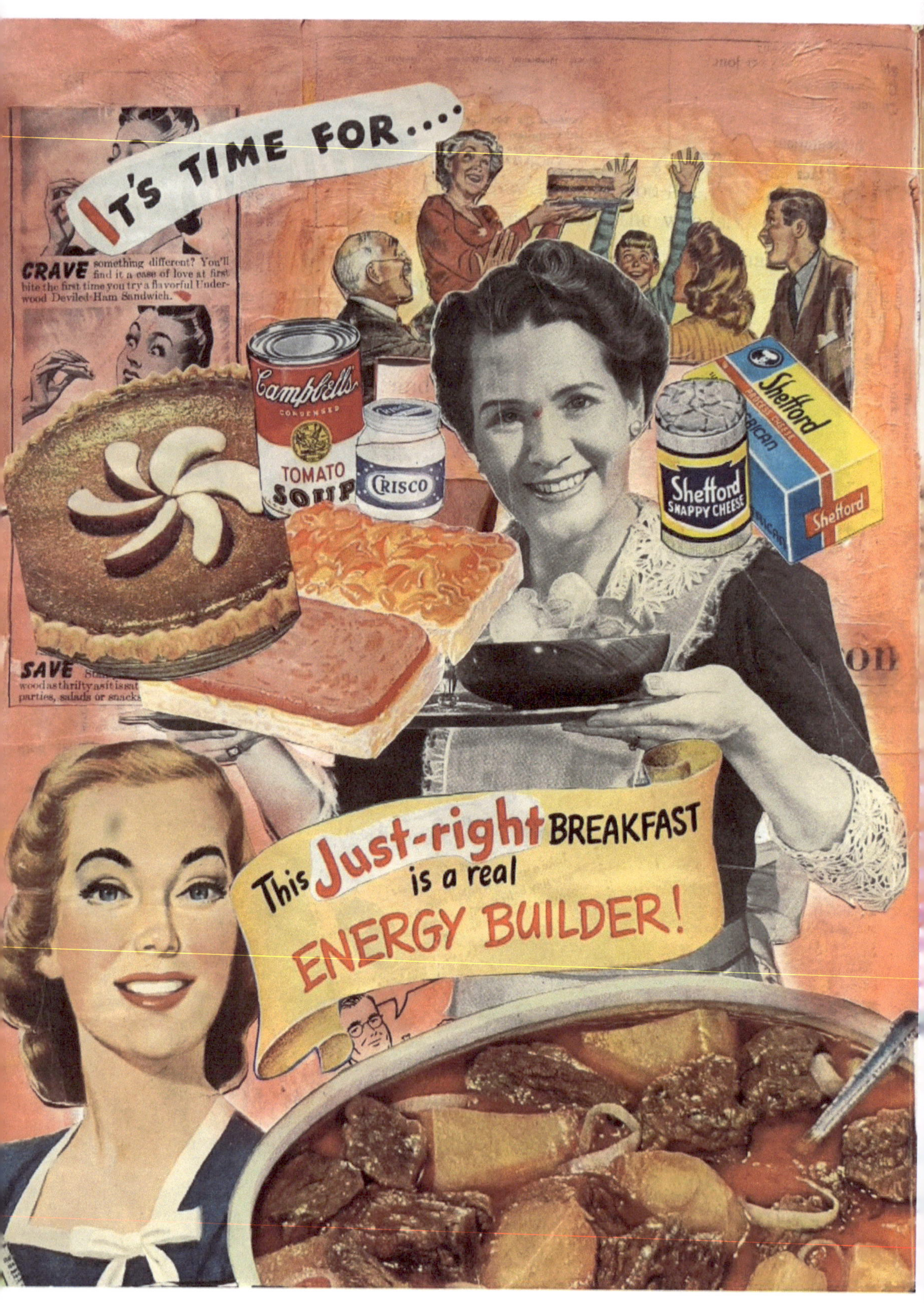
IT'S TIME FOR....
CRAVE something different? You'll find it a case of love at first bite the first time you try a flavorful Underwood Deviled-Ham Sandwich.
Campbell's
CONDENSED
TOMATO
SOUP
CRISCO
Shefford
SNAPPY CHEESE
Shefford
SAVE
This Just-right BREAKFAST
is a real
ENERGY BUILDER!

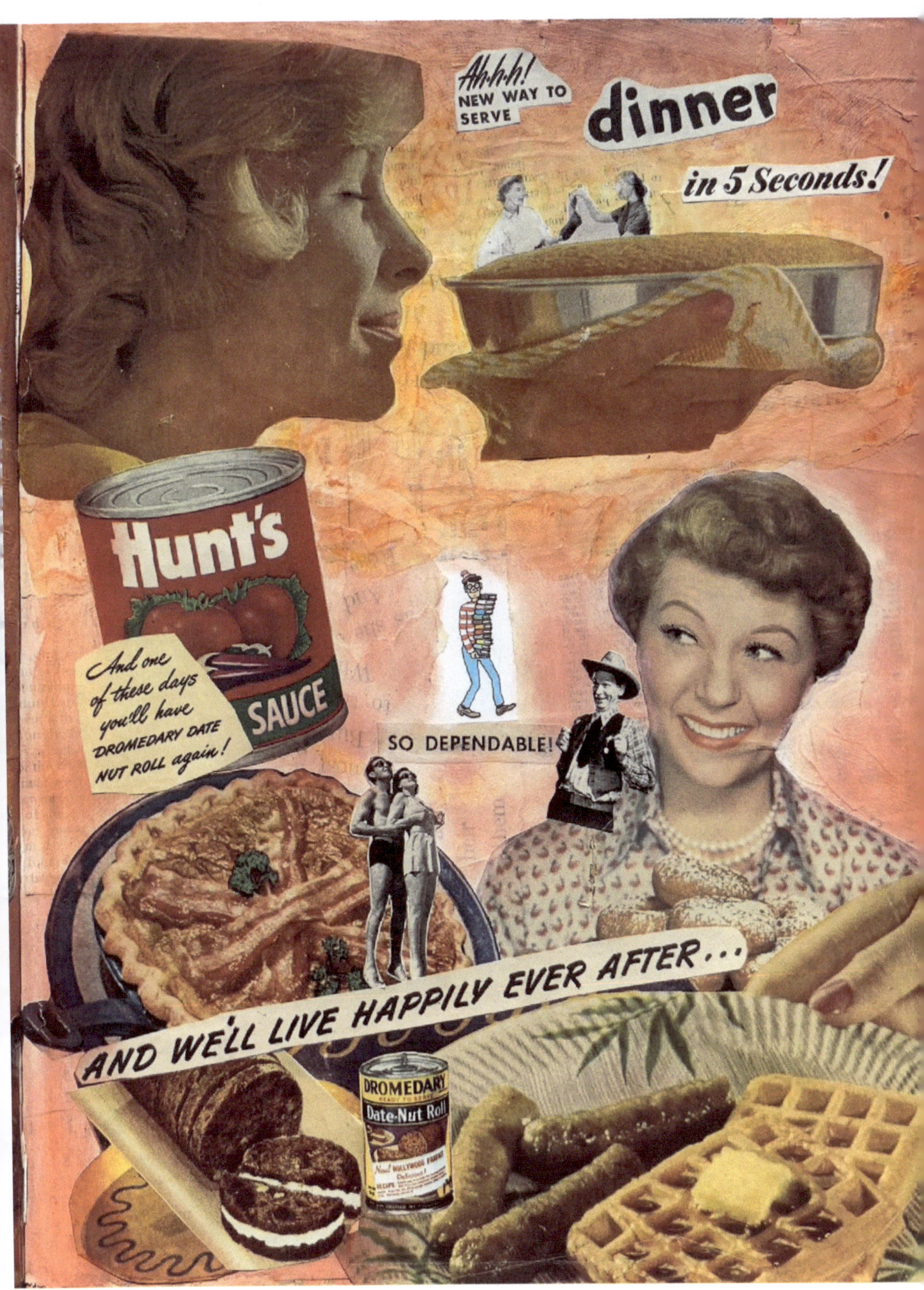
Ah-h-h!
NEW WAY TO SERVE
dinner
in 5 Seconds!
Hunt's
SAUCE
And one of these days you'll have DROMEDARY DATE NUT ROLL again!
SO DEPENDABLE!
AND WE'LL LIVE HAPPILY EVER AFTER...
DROMEDARY
Date-Nut Roll

www.ingramcontent.com/pod-product-compliance
Lightning Source LLC
LaVergne TN
LVHW070204110826
845147LV00002B/497

9780999122297